THE BASICS OF
MICROBES

CORE CONCEPTS

THE BASICS OF MICROBES

ANNE WANJIE, EDITOR

ROSEN
PUBLISHING®
New York

This edition published in 2014 by:

The Rosen Publishing Group, Inc.
29 East 21st Street
New York, NY 10010

Additional end matter copyright © 2014 by The Rosen Publishing Group, Inc.

Library of Congress Cataloging-in-Publication Data

Wanjie, Anne.
The basics of microbes/Anne Wanjie.—1st ed.—New York:
Rosen, © 2014
     p. cm.—(Core concepts)
Includes bibliographical references and index.
ISBN 978-1-4777-0550-6
1. Microorganisms—Juvenile literature. 2. Microbiology_Juvenile
literature. I. Title.
QR57 .W36 2014
576

Manufactured in the United States of America

CPSIA Compliance Information: Batch #S13YA: For further information, contact Rosen Publishing, New York, New York, at 1-800-237-9932.

© 2004 Brown Bear Books Ltd.

CONTENTS

CHAPTER 1: MICROSCOPIC LIFE   6

CHAPTER 2: WHAT ARE BACTERIA?   10

CHAPTER 3: WHAT ARE PROTISTS?   22

CHAPTER 4: WHAT ARE VIRUSES?   34

CHAPTER 5: THE CONNECTION
       BETWEEN MICROORGANISMS
       AND DISEASE   46

CHAPTER 6: USEFUL MICROORGANISMS   58

CHAPTER 7: BIOGRAPHY:
       LOUIS PASTEUR   73

GLOSSARY   88

FOR MORE INFORMATION   90

FOR FURTHER READING   91

INDEX   92

CHAPTER ONE

MICROSCOPIC LIFE

Rotting grapes. Bacteria cause the fruit to rot and decompose. The visible signs of mold on the surface of the grapes are the fruiting bodies of a parasitic fungus growing inside the fruit.

Microorganisms matter. Although we cannot see them without using a microscope, billions of microorganisms live all around us—on land, sea, and even deep underground.

Microorganisms live in all extremes, from near-boiling volcanic springs to frozen polar ice, and from high mountain peaks to ocean trenches. They also live on and in all plants and animals. Microorganisms are often simple life forms, but they are essential to life on Earth.

The main types of microorganisms are bacteria and protists. Bacteria are single-celled organisms. People often think of them as dangerous and disease-causing, but most are not harmful. Many types of

THE BASICS OF MICROORGANISMS

A microorganism is any life form so small that you cannot see it without a powerful microscope. The word is used most commonly to refer to single-celled organisms that belong to two main groups: the bacteria and the protists. Viruses, although they are not cells, may also be included, as well as some microscopic fungi such as yeasts. The study of microorganisms is called microbiology.

bacteria break down dead organic matter, including food inside peoples' stomachs.

Protists include green algae, amebas, slime molds, and many types of plankton (floating organisms). The group is very diverse and includes many organisms that are related only distantly. Some protists move around like tiny animals. Others seem more like plants. Yet others are plantlike and animal-like at various stages in their life.

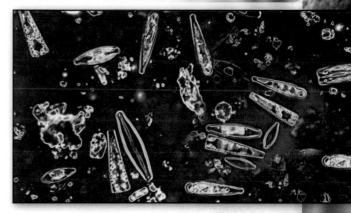

Diatoms are single-celled organisms that live in oceans. They have complex shapes formed by glassy skeletons with beautiful patterns.

WHY ARE MICROORGANISMS IMPORTANT?

Some microorganisms cause terrible diseases such as tuberculosis and AIDS. Yet overall, we cannot do without them. They are vital to all Earth's ecosystems, and life would be impossible without them.

Microorganisms are too small to see with the naked eye, so it is not always obvious how important they are. They play many different roles. Some microorganisms make their own food, as plants do. Others hunt prey, as animals do, while yet others rot down and recycle dead material. Plantlike microorganisms that float in the oceans are particularly important. Just like true plants, they use the energy in sunlight to turn water and carbon dioxide from the air into food and oxygen by photosynthesis. These microorganisms are eaten by others and form the base of a food chain that leads to fish, whales, and even people. Many single celled protists are plantlike. Plantlike protists are often called algae, or microalgae if they are single-celled.

AN INTERESTING DISCOVERY

In the 1700s the Dutch microscope-maker Anton van Leeuwenhoek (1632–1723) was the first person to see and describe many bacteria and protists. Detailed understanding of these life forms came much later, however. In the 19th century the French scientist Louis Pasteur (1822–1895) proved that rotting and fermentation processes were caused by microorganisms and provided strong evidence that they also caused disease.

Bacteria were first proved to cause diseases in humans and other animals by the German physician Robert Koch (1843–1910) in 1880. A better understanding of viruses, which are much smaller than bacteria, had to wait until the 20th century.

MICROSCOPIC COOPERATION

Microorganisms often team up with other living things in relationships called symbioses. Sometimes one partner is a parasite or a smaller creature that hitches a ride on a larger one. Often two creatures form a mutually beneficial relationship called a mutualism. For example, cattle have microorganisms in their gut that help them digest their tough plant food. The microorganisms get a safe home in return. Corals (right) are tiny animals that live in colonies and form coral reefs. They share a mutualism with single-celled algae in their tissues that supply them with much of their food.

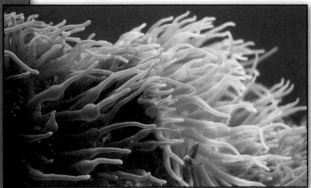

carrying out certain chemical reactions. For example, during the process called nitrogen fixation some bacteria in the soil and on the roots of plants take nitrogen from the air. They turn it into compounds that are used by plants. Plants could not grow without these bacteria.

Not all the microorganisms called algae are related closely.

BY-PRODUCTS

Some microorganisms—especially bacteria—are vital to the cycling of elements such as carbon and nitrogen through ecosystems. Although they are tiny and simple compared to animals and plants, bacteria are nature's experts at

LIFE IN EXTREME CONDITIONS

Microorganisms live everywhere on Earth, including some very extreme or difficult environments where other organisms cannot survive, such as places where there is no oxygen. Some bacteria live in water that is boiling hot or extremely salty. Others feed off chemicals that are poisonous to other organisms.

Most life on Earth is based on energy from the sun. Hydrothermal vents are

VIRUSES

Some scientists do not think viruses are life forms because viruses cannot obtain their own energy or grow and reproduce on their own. Viruses consist only of a piece of genetic material surrounded by a protein coat. They are parasites and reproduce by infecting living cells. Viral infections cause diseases such as influenza, smallpox, and AIDS (acquired immune deficiency syndrome).

YOU CAN MAKE COMPOST

Fill a wooden-framed container with a mixture of grass clippings, weeds, twigs, pieces of paper, and nonmeat food scraps. These items provide all the food needed by microorganisms. Create small pockets of air in the deeper layers by adding paper rolls, egg cartons, or similar items. Within a few days the mixture heats up as oxygen-using microorganisms start decomposing, or breaking down, the material.

Stir and water the mixture once every week to allow water and oxygen to penetrate the heap. If you are lucky, the microorganisms will reward you with a dark, crumbly soil-like compost in as little as eight weeks. You can use this stuff to fertilize or enrich the soil in your backyard. It is good to use because the bacteria have decomposed the original materials, so the nutrients they contained are available again.

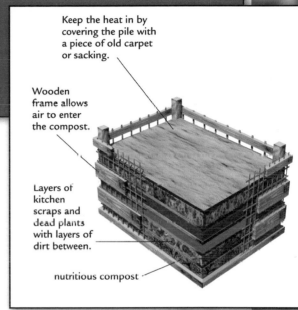

Keep the heat in by covering the pile with a piece of old carpet or sacking.

Wooden frame allows air to enter the compost.

Layers of kitchen scraps and dead plants with layers of dirt between.

nutritious compost

hot-water channels on the deep ocean floor. There, sulfur-using bacteria form the base of a food web that does not depend on sunlight at all.

The bacteria trap chemical energy from sulfides in the hot water that gushes from the vents just as plants do from sunlight. Other microorganisms live in less harsh environments but need to be able to survive occasional hard times. Many form a thick wall around themselves when they need to survive unfavorable conditions.

Microorganisms vary in size enormously from one type to another. They even form their own food chains; larger animal-like protists eat smaller microorganisms such as bacteria and algae.

MICROORGANISMS AND PEOPLE

Bread, wine, and cheese are all made with help from microorganisms. Industrial uses for microorganisms, or biotechnology, include the manufacture of drugs, solvents (dissolving liquids), and some types of plastics. Other uses include the spreading of insect-attacking proteins to control pests and using biological methods to clean up pollution.

Much of the knowledge scientists have gained in the fields of biochemistry, genetics, and molecular biology has come from studying bacteria and viruses. So too have many of the techniques used in genetic engineering.

CHAPTER TWO

WHAT ARE BACTERIA?

The colors in Morning Glory Pool in Yellowstone National Park are from pigments in thermophile bacteria. Thermophiles live at high temperatures. Some make energy from sulfur.

Some bacteria cause diseases, but most perform vital or useful functions—in the digestive systems of animals and also in the recycling of nitrogen.

There are more bacteria living on Earth than any other life form. They live in air, water, soil, and plants and animals. Evidence that bacteria may have been the first organisms on Earth comes from the fact that some bacteria live in harsh environments that are probably similar to the conditions present on Earth when life first began.

People usually think of bacteria as disease-causing germs. However, the bacteria that cause diseases such as cholera, tuberculosis, and the sexually transmitted disease gonorrhea make up just a tiny portion of the bacterial world.

We depend on bacteria for many important functions in life, including maintaining Earth's atmosphere as well as breaking down decaying matter and releasing the nutrients they contain

TYPES OF CELLS

All life forms except viruses have one of two sorts of cells, called prokaryote cells and eukaryote cells. Bacteria are prokaryotes; other life forms—plants, animals, fungi, and protists—are all types of eukaryotes. Prokaryotes have circular, double-stranded DNA as their genetic material. It floats freely within the cell and is not enclosed in a separate, membrane-bound nucleus (control center), as it is in the cells of eukaryote organisms.

back into the environment. They also digest food in the gut of animals.

Recycling Earth's nitrogen is another important bacterial activity. Plants need nitrogen to grow properly. Soil bacteria make nitrogen available to plants by changing nitrogen gas from the air into nitrates or nitrites in a process called nitrogen fixation.

MEASUREMENTS

Bacteria are among the smallest organisms on Earth. A human body has billions of cells, but each bacterium ("bacteria" is plural) is just one cell. A bacterium may be just a few nanometers long (a nanometer is 1 millionth of a millimeter) or as large as .03 in. (0.75 millimeters) in length. Bacteriologists (scientists who study bacteria) view bacteria through microscopes because they are too small to be seen with the naked eye. Bacteria are always single-celled, but some types join up and form filaments or threads. These threads may be visible to the naked eye. Even in bacteria that live in groups the contents of each cell remain separate.

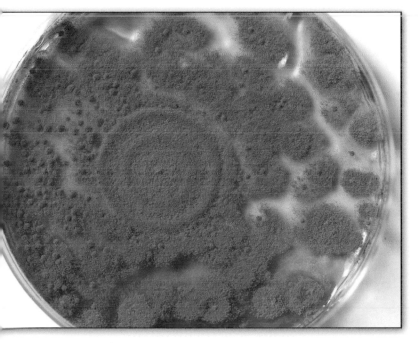

Bacteria growth can be plainly seen on the surface in this petri dish. An individual bacterium, however, would be too small to view without a microscope.

◀ **SPHERICAL BACTERIA,** *cocci* (singular is *coccum*), exist singly or as chains or blocks of cells.

▼ **ROD-SHAPED BACTERIA** are called *bacilli* (singular is *bacillus*).

▲ **COMMA-SHAPED BACTERIA** are curved rods called *vibrio*. They cause cholera.

◀ **SPIRAL BACTERIA** may be single or form chains.

Bacteria exist in different shapes but the three most common are rods, spheres, and spirals.

usually more than 100 times smaller. However, there are some exceptions: The relatively huge bacterium *Epulopiscium fischelsoni* is .02 in. (0.5 mm) long; it can just about be seen with the naked eye. This bacterium lives in the gut of the surgeon fish, where it feeds on the fish's digested food.

TYPES OF BACTERIA

Not long after bacteria appeared about 3.5 billion years ago, they split into two groups, archaebacteria and eubacteria. The groups are very different in terms of their structure and

A typical bacterial cell is much simpler than an animal or plant cell and is

FOOD BACTERIA

Bacteria are used widely in the food industry to ferment foods or alter their properties, making them more flavorsome, digestible, or merely to improve their texture. Fermentation is a natural chemical process in which microorganisms, such as bacteria and yeast (a fungus), get their energy by breaking down sugars to form alcohol and carbon dioxide gas in an oxygen-free environment. Dairy products, bread, vinegar, and pickled vegetables are some of the foods we enjoy every day thanks to bacteria. Milk is fermented to cheese, yogurt, and sour cream by the lactic acid-producing bacteria *Lactobacillus*, *Leuconostoc*, and *Streptococcus*. The bacteria change the taste and texture of the products and even help them keep better: Some cheeses can be stored for months at room temperature.

YOU CAN MAKE YOGURT

Grow some harmless bacteria using a pot of plain live yogurt (make sure it is not pasteurized). Look out for the name *Streptococcus thermophilus* on the label. You will also need skimmed milk powder, 2 measuring cups, 2 clean glass jars with lids, 2 forks, and hot water. Put 2 ounces (50g) of skimmed milk powder into each of the measuring cups, and label them A and B.

Using a fork, mix the powder with two-thirds of a pint (300ml) of hot water in each bowl. Then add a tablespoon of the plain yogurt to the milk in A. Ask an adult to rinse the jars with boiling water, and label them A and B. Put the mixture from bowl A into jar A and, so that you can make a comparison, from bowl B into jar B. Put the lids on the jars, and leave them in a warm place overnight. Then open the jars, and compare the contents. In jar A you should see plenty of freshly made yogurt, but there should be none in jar B. The bacteria in the starting yogurt feeds on the lactose sugar in the milk. The lactose becomes lactic acid, which curdles the milk and makes more yogurt.

metabolism (how they carry out their life processes). The name archaebacteria is misleading since eubacteria are more ancient ("archae" means old). Scientists have studied eubacteria—which include most of the known species of bacteria—much more thoroughly than archaebacteria.

Scientists have recognized about 5,000 different types of bacteria on Earth, but there may be millions more awaiting discovery. Bacteria exist in a variety of different shapes: rods, spheres, spirals, and commas (see left). Scientists mostly classify bacteria by their genetic (inherited) characteristics and by how they get their energy.

WHAT ARE ARCHAEBACTERIA?

Archaebacteria often live in environments that few other organisms can exploit. These habitats include salty places, inhabited by halophile (which means "salt-loving") bacteria, hot places, inhabited by thermophile ("heat-loving") bacteria, or environments that are low in oxygen such as the sand or mud of swamps, marshes, and estuaries. These are anaerobic (oxygen-hating) bacteria. People use anaerobic bacteria to decompose sewage and other waste. Similar types of bacteria live in the guts of animals, including people, where they break down food and so aid digestion.

Halophiles live in very salty environments, such as the Great Salt Lake in Utah. The bacteria contain high levels of pigments (coloring) and are purple or red. Extreme thermophiles live in very hot places, such as deep-ocean hydrothermal vents. *Sulfolobus* is a thermophile bacterium that lives in hot sulfur springs in Yellowstone National Park. It gets energy by breaking down sulfur compounds. Other thermophiles break down organic material.

WHAT ARE EUBACTERIA?

Biologists have used genetic studies to classify eubacteria into several main groups (see below). Eubacteria contain some species of bacteria that are necessary for maintaining Earth's atmosphere. For example, cyanobacteria produce oxygen and change nitrogen, an essential nutrient, into a form that can be used by other organisms. Cyanobacteria are among the most ancient kinds of bacteria. Their fossils are the oldest of any known life form. Biologists believe that oxygen-producing cyanobacteria changed Earth's atmosphere and so enabled oxygen-dependent organisms such as animals to evolve.

Different types of bacteria react differently to oxygen gas. Aerobic bacteria thrive in oxygen-rich environments. Like animals, aerobic bacteria need plenty of oxygen to respire (produce energy). Yet

GROUPS OF BACTERIA

Bacteria are divided into two main groups. They are the eubacteria and the archaebacteria. The eubacteria are the older group. Scientists are unsure when the archaebacteria split from the eubacteria. This major division may have taken place as long as 3 billion years ago, or it may have been much more recent; some scientists think the split took place around 850 million years ago. The two main bacteria groups are further separated into several major divisions, as shown in this chart.

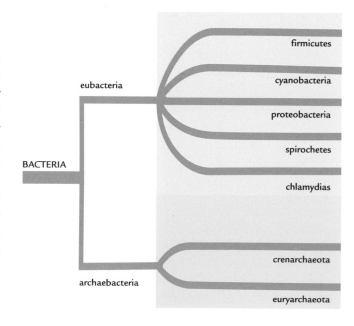

BACTERIAL GENETICS

Scientists have used genetic technology to find out about the relationship between bacteria and the eukaryotes. In all organisms the DNA gradually mutates (changes) over time. Therefore, closely related species have fewer mutations than more distantly related species. By studying differences in the DNA between eubacteria, archaebacteria, and eukaryotes, biologists have concluded that archaebacteria seem to be more closely related to eukaryotes than to eubacteria.

for anaerobic (oxygen-hating) bacteria oxygen gas is deadly poison. Anaerobic bacteria thrive in oxygen-free environments such as deep, wet mud. Not all bacteria are aerobic or anaerobic—some thrive in oxygen but can survive even when oxygen is scarce.

NUTRIENTS AND BACTERIA

Bacteria capture energy and nutrients in a variety of ways. Like all other organisms, they need energy and nutrients to grow and reproduce. Some bacteria consume energy-giving molecules such as

glucose, just as animals do. They are called heterotrophs. Typical heterotrophs include bacteria that live in and consume decaying matter.

Organisms that make their own energy are called autotrophs, or self-feeders. There are two main types of autotrophic bacteria: photoautotrophs, which make food using energy from sunlight, and chemoautotrophs, which use a similar process to make food from chemicals.

Photoautotrophic bacteria make food from carbon dioxide gas through a process

A sewage-treatment plant as viewed from above. After waste is filtered, bacteria feed on the liquid part and make it harmless. The bacteria are removed to be reused. Other bacteria feed on the crude sludge for three to four weeks.

called photosynthesis. Chemoautotrophs, such as *Sulfolobus*, make their own food in a similar way; but instead of sunlight, they use energy from chemicals. Many chemoautotrophs live on the ocean floor at depths of more than 6,500 feet (2km). These bacteria live in permanent darkness and rely for their nutrients on chemicals, such as sulfur, that are released from volcanic hydrothermal (hot-water) vents.

Some bacteria act as both heterotrophs and autotrophs. These bacteria not only eat food they encounter in the environment but also use sunlight or chemical energy to make their own food.

STRUCTURE OF BACTERIA

Bacteria are more simple than animal and plant cells. A bacterial cell is filled by a gel-like fluid called the cytoplasm. The cytoplasm is encased by a supple cell membrane that is, in turn, surrounded by a hardy and inflexible cell wall. The cell wall maintains the bacterium's shape. It also controls what can leave and enter the cell and so protects the bacterium against swelling and bursting. Eubacterial cell walls are strengthened by a thick network of fibers.

Some bacteria are protected further by a slimy capsule. The capsule helps keep bacteria from drying out or being destroyed by white blood cells, probably because it makes the bacterial cell slippery.

DNA OF BACTERIA

Animals and plants have a nucleus in their cells that contains genetic material in

STRUCTURE OF A BACTERIAL CELL

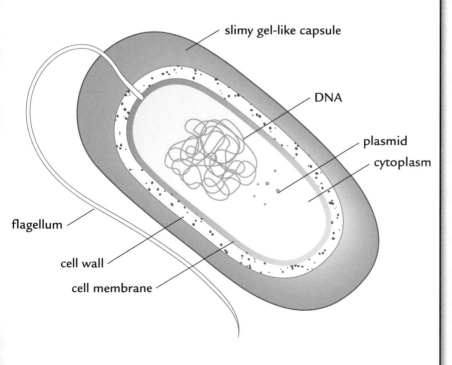

slimy gel-like capsule

DNA

plasmid

cytoplasm

flagellum

cell wall

cell membrane

A simple rod-shaped bacterium. An outer gel-like capsule protects the cell. The tough cell wall holds the bacteria's shape. A support membrane surrounds the cytoplasm, which contains the bacterium's DNA. Some DNA is also enclosed inside tiny packets called plasmids. The flagellum helps the bacterium move by whipping around.

BACTERIA AND THE GRAM STAIN

Bacteria are identified using a staining technique called the Gram stain, named after its developer Danish physician Hans Christian Gram (1853–1938). Gram-positive bacteria stain purple when exposed to the Gram stain. Gram-negative bacteria are not stained by the purple dye. The Gram stain reacts to differences in the structure of the bacterial cell surface. Bacteria with an outer layer that contains a chemical called peptidoglycan are Gram-positive. The peptidoglycan turns purple when exposed to the stain. Gram-negative bacteria have less peptidoglycan and a further outer membrane that keeps out the stain. Gram-negative bacteria can resist antibiotics (drugs that kill bacteria) thanks to the extra outer membrane.

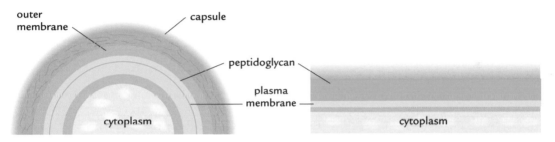

Gram-negative bacteria do not retain the violet dye when tested.

Gram-positive bacteria retain the violet dye and appear deep blue or purple.

the form of DNA. A key difference between these cells and bacterial cells is that bacterial cells have no nucleus. Bacterial DNA is held in the cytoplasm as a bare molecule in a loose clump. The clump is sometimes called the nuclear body or nucleoid. Unlike DNA of other organisms, bacterial DNA is not enclosed by a nuclear membrane.

In animal and plant cells the DNA molecule is attached to proteins, but bacterial DNA molecules are bare.

Many bacteria also have tiny circles of DNA called plasmids that contain just a

A crown gall on the base of a Chrysanthemum. The disease is caused by *Agrobacterium tumefaciens*, a Gram-negative rod-shaped bacterium that lives in the soil and plant roots.

few genes. Plasmids are not part of the main DNA, and they replicate (make copies of themselves) independently.

Archaebacterial DNA is not like that of other bacteria. Some archaebacteria have sections in their DNA called introns, or junk DNA. No one knows what the role of introns is, or even if they have a function at all. Other bacteria do not have introns, but many plant and animal cells (eukaryotes) do.

WHAT IS CYTOPLASM?

Animal and plant cells contain internal miniorgans called organelles. Organelles carry out functions such as energy production. Bacterial cells must perform similar functions, but they do so using less complex cell structures. Bacterial cytoplasm does not contain organelles except granules called ribosomes. They are the cell's protein-making machines.

RESISTANCE TO ANTIBIOTICS

Antibiotics are chemicals that fight infections by bacteria. Antibiotics have saved many lives and made many bacterial diseases a thing of the past. However, antibiotics have also been overused, and many bacteria have become resistant to them. As a result, diseases such as tuberculosis have started to become more common again. Doctors often prescribe antibiotics unnecessarily, and farmers give them to animals in vast quantities. Patients also increase bacterial resistance by not finishing their courses of antibiotics when their symptoms begin to improve, allowing the bacteria to survive and adapt.

Resistance builds up because bacteria reproduce very quickly, and mutations soon build up in a population. Some of these mutant (changed) bacteria can resist antibiotics. They pass on this ability to other bacteria by conjugation or binary fission, and resistance spreads.

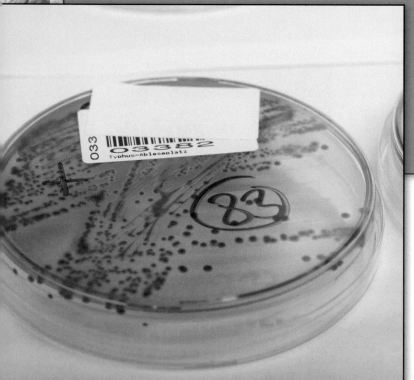

Escherichia coli, also known as *E. coli,* is shown growing in this petri dish. *E. coli* is one form of bacteria that can grow resistant to antibiotics.

In eukaryotes organelles called mitochondria produce energy through respiration. Plants have organelles called chloroplasts, which make energy from sunlight using photosynthesis. Bacteria generate their energy in the cytoplasmic membrane.

THE MOVEMENT OF BACTERIA

Bacteria can move in different ways depending on their features. Many have a tail-like structure called a flagellum. The flagellum spins around rapidly and propels the bacterium forward. Other bacteria move by producing a layer of slime and sliding around. Yet other bacteria have a series of filaments called fimbriae that stick out from the cell surface. Fimbriae enable the

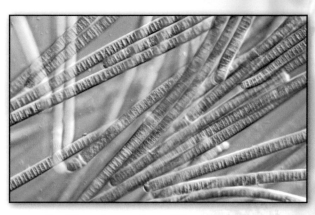

Oscillatoria are threadlike cyanobacteria that make stones slick in damp areas.

bacteria to grip surfaces and ease forward. Some bacteria contain tiny mineral particles that are sensitive to Earth's magnetic field. The particles act like a compass and help bacteria travel in a particular direction.

BACTERIAL REPRODUCTION

Organisms reproduce either by sexual or asexual reproduction. Sexual reproduction involves mixing the genes of two parents. Mixing of genes ensures that each generation is slightly different than its parent's.

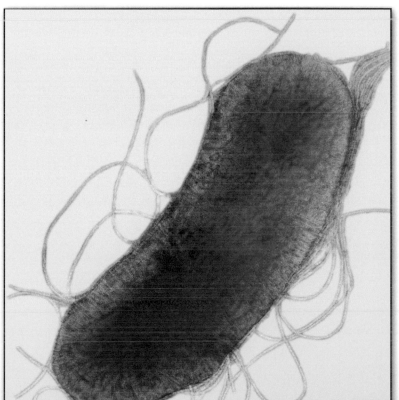

The slender, threadlike filaments coating this bacterium are called fimbriae. Fimbriae attach the bacterium to a surface or keep it in close contact with another cell, such as one in an animal's gut.

REPRODUCTION OF BACTERIA

1

bacterial cell

2

DNA

3

daughter cell

daughter cell

4

Binary fission is a method of asexual reproduction. The DNA inside a bacterial cell (1) replicates, then the cell divides (2). Each daughter cell contains identical DNA (3). The process happens again with each daughter cell to make four (4). Bacterial populations increase rapidly as the reproductive process goes on in this way.

Asexual reproduction involves only one parent—for example, when a cutting from a plant grows into a new individual. There is no mixing of genes during asexual reproduction, and little genetic (inherited) variation is introduced during the process.

Bacteria reproduce by a type of asexual reproduction called binary fission. One cell splits and forms two identical daughter cells. The daughter cells divide, producing cells that also divide, and so on. Binary fission gives populations of bacteria the potential to double every 20 minutes.

Each time a cell divides, there are likely to be small errors in copying its DNA. These errors are called mutations. Rapid reproduction, such as that of bacteria, leads quickly to a buildup of mutations over the

generations. Mutations enable bacteria to evolve speedily into new types.

Some bacteria can introduce further variation into their genetic information by exchanging genes with nearby bacteria through a process called conjugation. During conjugation a bacterium produces a hairlike structure, called a pilus, that attaches to a neighboring bacterium. A piece of DNA moves from one bacterium to the other along the pilus. In this way genes that aid survival, such as those that provide antibiotic resistance, can move between bacteria. Infecting viruses also introduce genetic material into bacteria.

DISEASE-CAUSING BACTERIA

All bacteria that cause disease are types of eubacteria. Some invade tissues, as is

PENICILLIN

Like many scientific breakthroughs, the discovery of penicillin was accidental. Its discoverer was Alexander Fleming (1881–1955), a Scotsman working in London. Fleming's lab was a jumble of bottles and equipment. In 1928 Fleming went on vacation and left his bacterial culture plates unwashed. When he came back, he noticed that a mold had grown on one of the plates. The mold was secreting a substance that killed off the bacteria around it. He named the substance penicillin.

Fleming experimented further but was unable to purify the penicillin. Other scientists managed this in the early 1940s, and by the end of World War II (1939–1945) penicillin was saving the lives of soldiers injured in battle. Fleming, along with the scientists who developed the drug, was awarded the Nobel Prize for Medicine in 1945.

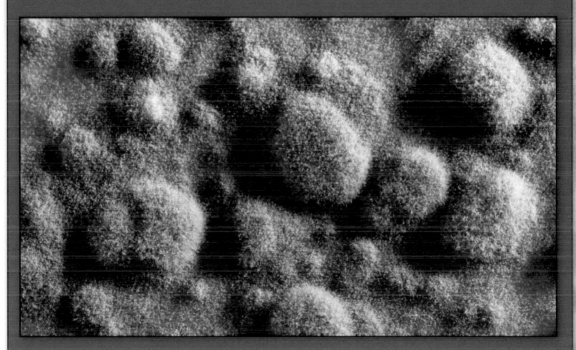

Penicillium mold, from which the drug penicillin is extracted.

the case in tuberculosis, a disease that can be deadly. Others produce dangerous toxins that affect the victim. *Vibrio cholerae*, for example, produces a toxin that causes a deadly disease called cholera. *Salmonella* has toxins in its outer membranes that cause severe food poisoning.

CHAPTER THREE

WHAT ARE PROTISTS?

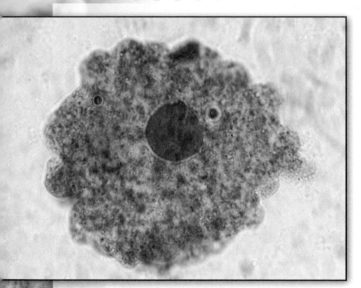

Amebas are single-celled protists that change their shape to move around. Their "limbs" are temporary extensions called pseudopodia, or false feet: To move, an ameba extends fingerlike projections of itself in the direction of travel. Then, the ameba's insides flow into its false feet, extending them even more. This drags the cell forward, enabling the ameba to crawl around.

The protist kingdom is largely made up of microorganisms, including amebas, single-celled algae, and slime molds. Seaweeds are also part of the group. Some protists live as plankton and are vital to the world's ecosystems. Others are parasites and can be dangerous.

The ameba is probably one of the most famous of all microorganisms. This crawling, blob-shaped creature has long been used as a symbol of primitive life, but amebas are specialized, highly adapted organisms. They are members of the kingdom Protista, or protists, a varied group of mainly single-celled life forms. From the countless microscopic inhabitants of the world's oceans to dangerous organisms such as the malaria parasite, protists are hugely important members of the world's ecosystems.

STRUCTURE AND EVOLUTION

Around two billion years ago on Earth a major event took place—the appearance

CLASSIFYING PROTISTS

In the past biologists thought that all organisms could be classified as either animals or plants. When it came to single-celled life forms, all green plantlike ones were called *algae*, and all animal-like ones *protozoa*. However, this classification was oversimplified since many single-celled organisms did not fit neatly into one group.

As long ago as the 1860s, *protist* was suggested for microorganisms that were neither plant nor animal. But it was not until after 1960 that the protists became a kingdom. Until recently, the protist kingdom was also called the kingdom Protoctista, but *protoctist* is no longer used. *Algae* is still used as a general term, however, although it is no longer used in scientific classifications. *Protozoan* still describes and classifies animal-like protists. This subkingdom's members are not all related, though.

of the first eukaryotic cells. Eukaryotic cells all have membrane-bound nuclei (singular, nucleus; the cell's control center). All plants, animals, fungi, and protists

COLLECT YOUR OWN PROTISTS

You can easily look at microlife that can develop in even the smallest puddle.

1. Make an artificial puddle by filling a clear jar about two-thirds full with cold water.

2. Tear up some decayed and fresh leaves and grass. Push them down into the water. Drop in a handful of soil. Carefully shake or stir the jar to mix up the contents.

3. Leave the jar to stand near a sunny window. After three weeks the water will be teeming with microorganisms that you can look at with a magnifying glass.

What can you see?
• A gold or brown mat at the bottom is made of diatoms.
• Slimy patches at the bottom are probably protozoans.
• Green algae turn the water green or are visible as long, thin threads on surfaces.
• Flagellate algae turn the water pinkish.

1–2

3

TYPES OF PROTISTS

▼ AMEBAS

Animal-like, constantly changing shape as they move; not all closely related; some types build protective cases.

▼ FLAGELLATES

This large grouping includes many unrelated types of protists; includes any with a flagella, including the dinoflagellates and euglenoids; can be animal-like or plantlike.

▼ EUGLENOIDS

flagellum

Single-celled flagellates. Some can switch from

making their own food to eating other cells; their relatives include the trypanosome parasites that cause sleeping sickness.

▼ DINOFLAGELLATES

Protists with two flagella (long whiplike structures used for movement; singular flagellum) and a protective armor of cellulose; important in plankton and red tides; both animal-like and plantlike features.

▼ CILIATES

cilia

Animal-like protozoans covered with many small hairlike projections of the cell membrane (cilia; singular cilium); among the most complex of all single-celled organisms; includes *Paramecium*.

▼ DIATOMS*

Plantlike protists that build intricate boxlike protective cases of silica (a glasslike material); important in plankton, the community of tiny drifting life forms of oceans and lakes that often forms the base of food chains.

▼ SPOROZOANS

Traditional grouping of many parasitic protists, including the malaria parasite *Plasmodium* (above).

▼ FORAMINIFERANS
(forams for short)

Animal-like, mainly marine; live in both

plankton and on seafloor; build elaborate protective cases, usually from chalky calcium carbonate.

▼ GREEN ALGAE*

Plantlike forms, especially important in fresh water; includes single-celled species, larger seaweeds, and filamentous (threadlike) *Spirogyra*. They are the ancestors of land plants.

▼ RADIOLARIANS* & HELIOZOANS

Protists usually with a spherical, radiating shape; not all closely related; heliozoans ("sun" animals) are mainly freshwater, while radiolarians are mainly marine.

*Protists that are generally referred to as types of microalgae (single-celled algae).

MINIATURE STRUCTURES

Many protists have complex internal or external skeletons, ranging from the flexible coverings (pellicles) of ciliates to elaborate rigid structures, often beautifully symmetrical. Diatoms and radiolarians build themselves skeletons of silica. (Silica is the material from which sand and glass are both made.)

Foraminiferans usually build their complex skeletons, or tests, out of calcium carbonate. Limestone and chalk are largely made up of foraminiferan tests. Forams might also use surrounding material, such as the bodies of other protists. Many types of amebas also build or secrete protective shells.

are made up of such cells. The first life forms consisted of cells similar to some bacteria that exist now (the eubacteria and archaea). Different prokaryote cells combined to form the first eukaryote cells. Over millions of years eukaryote cells combined and evolved into multicellular organisms such as animals and plants. Many eukaryote cells kept a simpler form and are now protists.

Protists include many life forms that are related only distantly to each other. The best definition of kingdom Protista is that it

consists of all eukaryotic life forms not classified as animals, plants, or fungi. Although most protists are single celled, some join together to form strands or colonies. The protist group also includes seaweeds such as kelp, which may grow up to 200 feet (60m) long. Not all the

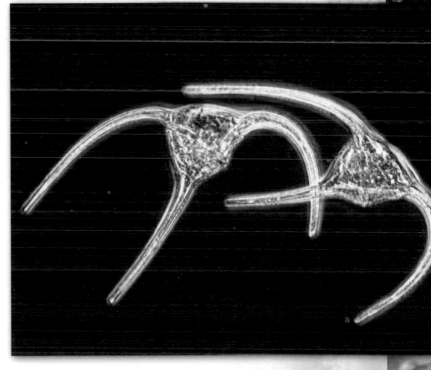

Dinoflagellate plankton have two flagella for propelling themselves. The flagella lie close to the body and are often hard to see. They are not visible in this photo. Dinoflagellates range in size from about 0.0002 to 0.08 inches (5 to 2,000 micrometers).

FEEDING A CILIATE

Ciliates have the most complex feeding apparatus of all protists. Most ciliates have the equivalent of a mouth and an anus; some even have a well-defined passage between the two, all within a single cell. Some ciliates can stretch their mouths to swallow prey that is much bigger than themselves.

single-celled species are microscopic: Various types can just be seen with the naked eye, while some deep-sea forms can be several inches across.

PROTIST LIFE

Just like more complex life forms, protists face the basic problems of getting food,

reproducing, and protecting themselves from predators and the environment. The difference for protists is that in most cases, each of these challenges has to be met by a single cell living on its own. Many protists seal themselves with a protective coating if conditions are unfavorable. They can survive for years within their protective coat.

WHAT THEY EAT

Protists can be classed as plantlike, animal-like, and funguslike depending on how they get their food. Plantlike forms include green algae, diatoms, about half the species of dinoflagellates, and several other groups. Like plants, these protists photosynthesize. Photosynthesis is the production of food from water and carbon dioxide, using the sun's energy.

WHAT IS BIOLUMINESCENCE?

When they detect water movement, some protists that live underwater emit light. This is called bioluminescence. It is a response to potential nighttime predators. By glowing, the protists reveal a predator to other creatures that might attack it. Can you think of any other ways that bioluminescence might be used by these and other underwater organisms?

The jellyfish in this aquarium show off their colors. Bioluminescence is used by jellyfish to scare away predators and also for mating.

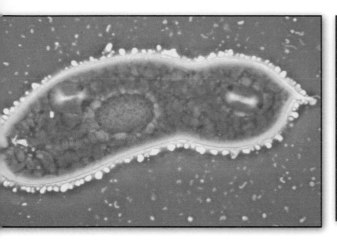

This *Euglena* is a protist with both plantlike and animal-like features. It contains chloroplasts for photosynthesis but can also eat other cells if the light fails. A *Euglena* cell measures between 0.0006 and 0.02 inches (15 and 500 micrometers) long.

Photosynthesizing protists contain chloroplasts. These organelles (mini-organs within cells) contain the green pigment chlorophyll, which traps the energy in sunlight. Green algae have the same chlorophyll as plants. Other protists, such as red algae (types of seaweeds), contain different chlorophylls and pigments of other colors that help them trap energy from the sun in low-light environments.

DEFENSE

Some protists have weapons that can be used both to attack prey and to defend themselves. *Paramecium* and other ciliates fire harpoonlike devices called trichocysts from under their cell surface. Trichocysts come in several varieties. Some anchor cells while feeding. Others even inject poison into neighboring cells.

Some animal-like protists filter tiny food particles from the water using sticky mucus or sievelike hairs. Others are able to swallow much larger particles whole. Amebas, for example, change their shape to create extensions called pseudopods (false feet) that reach out to surround their prey. They also use the pseudopods to move along: Stretching out a pseudopod allows the rest of the ameba's body to flow into it. Food particles are taken into the cell inside food vacuoles, which are small membrane-bound containers that work like temporary stomachs to digest the food. Animal-like protists can eat other protists, bacteria, small multicelled animals, and eggs of larger creatures.

WHAT ARE FOSSILS?

The fossils of shelled protists such as foraminiferans and radiolarians pile up at the bottom of the sea, forming limestone rocks. If sea levels change, the rocks are exposed as cliffs. Scientists learn about the sea millions of years ago from tiny protist fossils. Skeletons of diatoms at the bottom of a lake can provide information about its history.

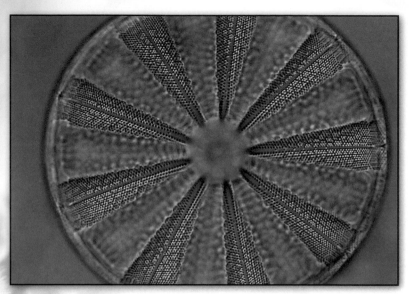

Diatoms are a major source of the oxygen in our air. As a protist such as this diatom photosynthesizes, it releases oxygen as a by-product.

HOW THEY MOVE

Many single-celled protists—even the plantlike ones—can move around. Some protists swim using long whiplike flagella or shorter cilia. Flagella move protists along by whipping around like a crocodile's tail; hairlike cilia ripple like waves and create a current. Flagella and cilia are extensions of the cell membrane. A few protists use ciliated bacteria stuck to their outside to do their swimming for them. Nonswimming protists move in various ways: Some wriggle along like worms; some glide smoothly using mucus, a slippery substance; and others make false feet.

MOVEMENT OF PHOTOSYNTHESIZING PROTISTS

Photosynthesizing protists need to stay near the water's surface to get enough sunlight. Often these protists have long spines that keep them from sinking, and some secrete oil droplets that help them

GENETICS AND REPRODUCTION

Sexual reproduction creates offspring with genetic (inherited) material that is a mix of both parents'. Genetic variation enables organisms to adapt to their environment. Many protists can reproduce sexually. Generally, they produce (or turn into) sex cells that fuse to form a fertilized cell. That cell becomes a new individual. Ciliates are unusual: Two cells come together, and each cell's nucleus (control center) divides in half. The nuclei contain DNA, which carries a cell's genes. Each parent cell sends one half of its nucleus to the other cell—the ciliates have mixed their genes. Both parent cells divide in half once to produce a total of four daughter cells. These cells are genetically different from either parent.

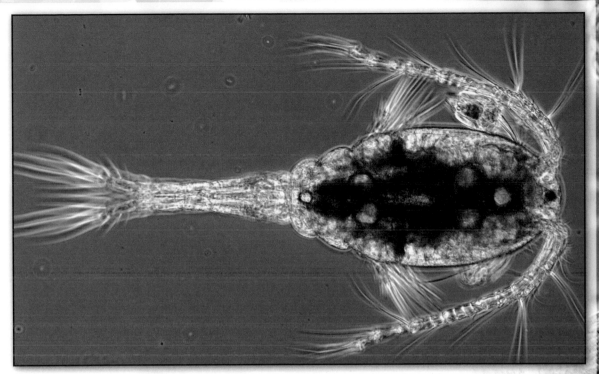

This copepod is a member of the zooplankton community. It is shown here many times bigger than it really is. Zooplankton are generally tiny animals, such as copepods and the larvae (young) of fish and shrimps. Many zooplankton feed on phytoplankton ("plantlike plankton"). The most numerous and important members of the phytoplankton are protists, including diatoms, dinoflagellates, radiolarians, and heliozoans. A copepod can catch a single protist cell in a tiny package of water. The copepod uses tiny hairs on its limbs to sweep algal cells into "bubbles" of water.

float. Some protists also have light-sensitive spots that enable the cells to detect and swim toward the sunlight. Attached, nonplanktonic protists often grow stalks for holding onto surfaces.

REPRODUCTION OF PROTISTS

The most common form of reproduction for single-celled protists is simple cell division. Sometimes the cell divides into two equal halves, forming identical offspring called daughter cells. In other cases a small bud is produced that detaches from the main cell and grows into a new cell. Some protist cells split into many small offspring at once.

If the cell has an external skeleton, one daughter cell may get to keep all of it, or it may be split and shared equally, depending on the species. These are all examples of asexual reproduction, since only one parent is involved, and the offspring are identical to the parent cell.

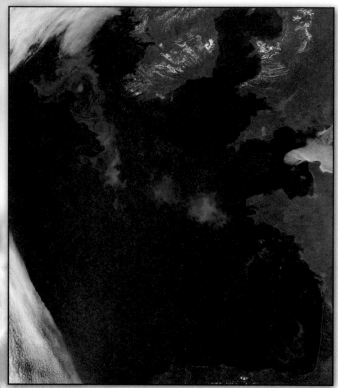

The bright blue-green patch in this satellite photograph of the North Atlantic ocean is a plankton bloom.

PROTISTS AND THE ECOSYSTEM

Protists—especially microscopic species—play a crucial part in the world's ecosystems. They abound in the sea, fresh water, the soil, and attached to or covering other living organisms. Some types of protists thrive in low-oxygen conditions, such as waterlogged mud. Others grow inside rocks in deserts or within solid blocks of ice.

Protists play a vital role as part of the plankton. Diatoms, dinoflagellates, and other plantlike protists use sunlight to generate the food on which most types of marine organisms depend.

Many protists get eaten by other protists such as ciliates or by small animals. In turn these animals become food for other creatures right up the food chain to large fish.

How well plantlike protists grow depends on the supply of nutrients in the water, especially nitrogen and

THE CHALLENGE OF FRESHWATER PROTISTS

Protists live in both fresh water and the sea. Among the plantlike protists green algae are mainly a freshwater group, while dinoflagellates are mainly a marine group. A particular challenge for green algae is that fresh water is much more dilute than their cell contents: There is a danger that water will enter the cell membrane by osmosis and make the cell swell up and burst. Osmosis is the movement of water across a semipermeable membrane from a weak solution to a strong one (a semipermeable membrane allows only some molecules to pass through it). Many freshwater protists overcome this using a contractile vacuole. This tiny saclike structure collects fresh water inside the animal and empties it to the outside.

WHAT IS CHAGAS' DISEASE?

Trypanosomes are tiny single-celled protists shaped a bit like worms. Their wormlike shape makes movement through the seas of blood cells, mud, or feces they live in easier. Trypanosomes cause several deadly diseases, including sleeping sickness and Chagas' disease. The parasites that cause Chagas' disease live inside insects called kissing bugs. Kissing bugs feed on blood. Sometimes a bug bites a person on the face while he or she is asleep (right). As the bug feeds, it often defecates on the person's skin. The deadly trypanosomes lurk in the bug's feces. The parasites are rubbed into the wound if the victim scratches the bite. Once inside the body, the parasites attack the heart and nervous system. More than 50,000 people die each year from Chagas' disease in South and Central America.

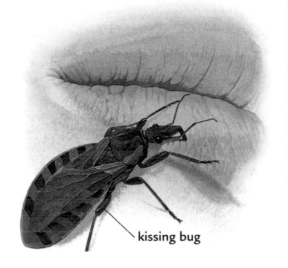

kissing bug

phosphorus compounds. Cool, temperate seas such as the North Atlantic are usually better "growing" regions than hot, tropical ones. That is because winter storms and ocean currents mix up the water and recycle nutrients. In spring there is often a great burst of plankton growth. It can create visible cloudlike blooms of algae.

SYMBIOSES

Many protists live in close relationships, or symbioses, with other types of organisms. Often both partners in such a relationship benefit. For example, flagellates that can break down wood live inside the guts of termites. Without their protist partners these insects would not be able to digest their wood-chip diet.

In other cases one protist lives inside another protist or even a larger animal. For example, many planktonic radiolarians engulf smaller plantlike protists, which stay alive inside the host. Many green algae and dinoflagellates live inside relatively large animals such as clams or corals. Reef-building corals rely on dinoflagellates called zooxanthellae, which live in corals' tissues. These protists help the coral build reefs and provide some of the coral's food. Environmental stresses such as pollution or an increase in water temperature can cause corals to lose their protist partners and die. This is called coral bleaching.

HOW IS MALARIA TRANSMITTED?

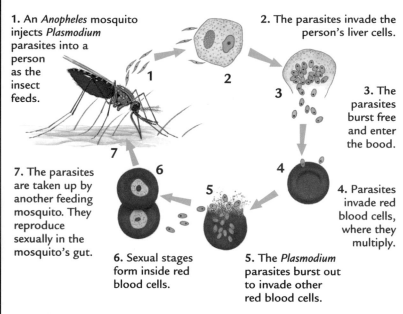

1. An *Anopheles* mosquito injects *Plasmodium* parasites into a person as the insect feeds.

2. The parasites invade the person's liver cells.

3. The parasites burst free and enter the bood.

4. Parasites invade red blood cells, where they multiply.

5. The *Plasmodium* parasites burst out to invade other red blood cells.

6. Sexual stages form inside red blood cells.

7. The parasites are taken up by another feeding mosquito. They reproduce sexually in the mosquito's gut.

Female *Anopheles* mosquitoes swallow a blood meal just before they lay a batch of eggs. If a *Plasmodium*-infected female feeds on a person's blood, the mosquito passes (transmits) the malarial parasite to that person.

PARASITES AND DISEASE

Sometimes the relationship between a protist and its partner is parasitic: The protist lives in or on a host organism, at the expense of the host. Many protists are parasites of plants, animals, or even other types of protists. Some do little damage as they steal food from and live within an animal's digestive system. Others live inside the cells or tissues of their hosts. These protists can sometimes cause serious diseases.

Only a few protists cause human diseases, but they include major killers such as malaria, Chagas' disease, and sleeping sickness. Other dangerous protists include an ameba that causes dysentery (a disease that affects the intestines) and a flagellate called *Trichomonas*, which infects reproductive organs.

Malaria has been a human disease for thousands of years. The name *malaria* comes from the Latin for "bad air." In the past people believed that the foul air in the low-lying, swampy places where malaria is most common was the cause of the disease. In reality mosquitoes breeding in the swamps were transmitting the disease

WHAT ARE TOXIC BLOOMS?

Some protists can cause serious illness without infecting an individual. Most notorious are ailments associated with the red tides that can occur along seashores in areas like Florida and California. These tides are caused by huge concentrations of dinoflagellates present in such numbers that they discolor the water. Some of these protists produce extremely toxic nerve poisons. The poisons build up in other animals that eat them, such as clams and oysters, which filter food from the water. People who eat the poisoned shellfish can become extremely ill.

This human red blood cell is shown infected with the malarial parasite *Plasmodium*. Malaria is spread to humans by species of tropical mosquitoes.

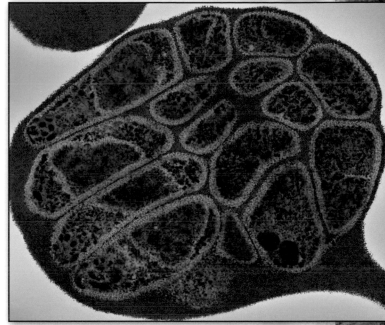

to people. This was finally proved by medical researchers in 1898.

Malaria is still the world's most serious infectious disease, killing more than two million people each year in the tropics, many of them children. The malarial parasite is called *Plasmodium*. It has a complex life cycle. *Plasmodium* reproduces sexually within the tissues of certain mosquitoes. It is then transferred to humans when the mosquito takes a blood meal. Once inside the human body, *Plasmodium* multiplies by dividing within liver and blood cells. The symptoms of malaria are severe fevers and chills that often recur.

African sleeping sickness, or trypanosomiasis, is caused by a trypanosome that lives in tropical parts of Africa. It also has a complex life cycle with several stages. The trypanosome lives within mammals such as cows. It can be transmitted to humans by the bite of bloodsucking tsetse flies. Sleeping sickness causes uncontrollable drowsiness and is often fatal. Another trypanosome parasite causes Chagas' disease in North and South America.

Scientists are trying to find vaccines to control malarial and trypanosomal diseases. So far, however, the protists have proved resistant to any vaccines. People who visit countries where malaria is a problem take drugs that kill the malarial parasites. If the drugs are taken for long periods, however, they damage a person's health and so cannot be taken by residents. Also, the parasites have developed resistance to the drugs.

CHAPTER FOUR

WHAT ARE VIRUSES?

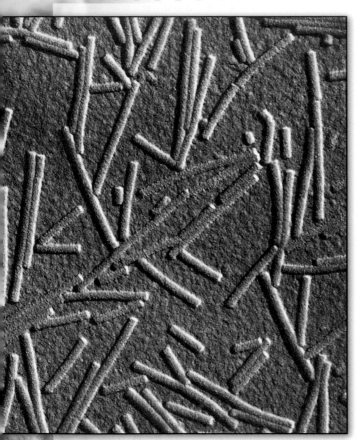

An electron micrograph of tobacco mosaic viruses (TMV) magnified many thousands of times. This virus was the first to be discovered by scientists, in 1892.

Viruses are simple structures made of pieces of genetic material (DNA or RNA) surrounded by a protein coat. Some scientists do not think viruses are living organisms.

Viruses are best known for causing major human diseases such as small-pox, yellow fever, and AIDS (acquired immune deficiency syndrome). However, these tiny parasitic life forms affect the entire natural world—animals, plants, bacteria, and fungi all live their lives at constant risk from viral attack.

Viruses are far smaller than single-celled organisms such as bacteria and protists. Unlike those organisms, viruses are not cells at all but consist of little more than a set of genetic (inherited) instructions packaged up in a protective protein coat. Viruses are very small, and they cannot grow and reproduce on their own. Instead, they have to get inside cells and take control of them, forcing the cells to switch to making viruses instead of carrying out their normal functions. Such cells are called host cells.

WHERE DID VIRUSES COME FROM?

Although viral diseases such as smallpox have been known since ancient times, people did not understand about viruses until much later. Toward the end of the 19th century researchers discovered that some disease-causing agents passed through fine filters that would trap bacteria. They called these tiny unknown life forms filterable viruses, later shortened to viruses. From the 1930's onward, after the electron microscope was invented, people could see what viruses really looked like.

No one is sure where viruses came from, especially since there are no fossils to help us trace their history. They may have originated in more than one way. Large, complex viruses such as poxviruses, for example, may have started off as cells that became parasitic and eventually lost many of their functions. Other viruses may have begun as pieces of a cell's machinery that later took on a life of their own. Some biologists think viruses come from outer space, but there is no proof of this.

Biology books sometimes say that viruses are not truly living. Outside living cells they are mostly inert—they show no biochemical activity. They can even be made into crystals and stored. On the other hand, their behavior is like that of some other parasites because they have adaptations—adjustments to environmental conditions—that allow them to spread and reproduce in their hosts.

Viruses have become very important in modern biology. Many basic discoveries about

Human immunodeficiency virus (or HIV) causes acquired immune deficiency syndrome (AIDS) by attacking white blood cells. It disables the immune system. Its core contains RNA, and it is surrounded by a protein shell.

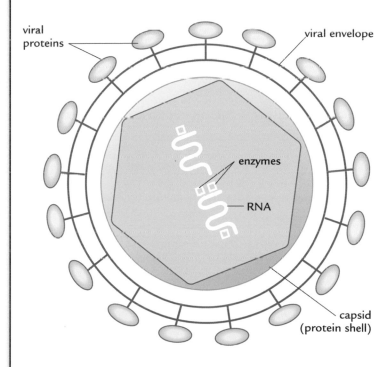

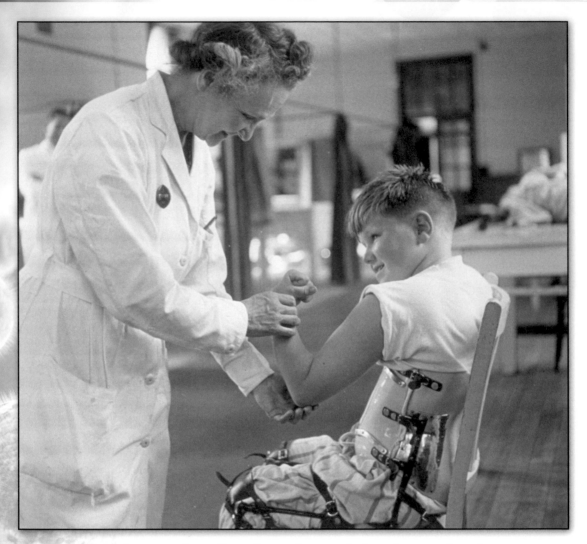

This 1947 photo shows a polio sufferer flexing his muscle for a doctor. A harmless gut virus, poliovirus can cause paralysis if it infects the nervous system.

VIROIDS

Some life forms are even smaller than viruses. Given the name viroids, these forms consist of a single RNA molecule folded into a complex three-dimensional shape. Viroids do not even have a protein coat to protect them. They are still a bit of a mystery, but they can cause various diseases in plants, which result in misshapen potatoes and dimpled apples. Scientists do not yet know whether viroids infect animals.

how cells and genes (segments of DNA that create physical characteristics) work have been made by studying viruses; they have also been vital in the development of genetic engineering techniques.

CLASSIFICATION OF VIRUSES

It has not been easy to figure out how viruses are related to each other, although studying the full sequences of their genes is providing some new clues. The information that has been used traditionally includes the size and shape of the organism, and whether the virus contains DNA (deoxyribonucleic acid) or RNA (ribonucleic acid). Currently, scientists divide viruses into about 70 families. Animal viruses range from the poxvirus family (the smallpox virus and its relatives), which are large DNA-containing viruses, to the picornavirus family, which are tiny RNA viruses that include the poliovirus and most viruses that cause colds.

Viruses exist in many shapes and sizes. The core of a virus consists of one or two strands of genetic material (either DNA or RNA). This material contains all the instructions (genes) for making new viruses. A protein coat called the capsid encloses the genetic material. Some viruses have an envelope made up of membranes, carbohydrates, and proteins. It surrounds the capsid.

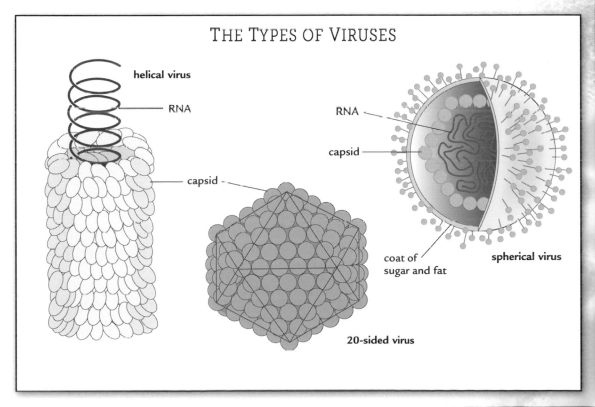

THE TYPES OF VIRUSES

helical virus
RNA
RNA
capsid
capsid
coat of sugar and fat
spherical virus
20-sided virus

STRUCTURE OF A VIRUS

At the heart of any virus is a set of genes, which are the instructions for all its life processes and for making more of the same virus. Unlike all other life forms, many viruses carry their genes as RNA, not DNA.

The number of viral genes ranges from only 3 or 4 up to 200 or more, depending on the type of virus. A simple organism such as a worm has tens of thousands of genes.

At the minimum a virus needs one or more genes that are the instructions to make its coat proteins plus others that tell a cell to make more copies of the virus. In all viruses the core genes are protected by a protein shell called a capsid.

A capsid's individual protein molecules fit together like the pieces of a jigsaw puzzle. The overall shape they take is usually either a long cylinder or else a compact 20-sided shape called an icosahedron. The AIDS virus is spherical. Some viruses also have an outer membrane and other structures, giving them a less regular shape.

The exact shape and chemical composition of the outer surface of a virus is usually unique for each type of virus. The capsid often helps the virus detect whether or not it has found the right host cell to invade. However, it also enables the host body to detect particular viruses, allowing defenses to be mounted against viral attack.

HOW DO VIRUSES REPRODUCE?

Viruses cannot swim or crawl around, so they have to rely on other ways of getting to their target cells. After arriving at the

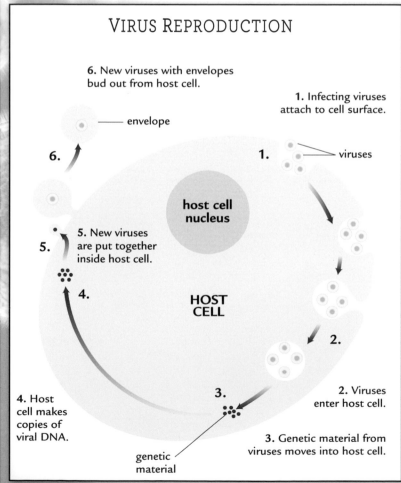

VIRUS REPRODUCTION

6. New viruses with envelopes bud out from host cell.

1. Infecting viruses attach to cell surface.

envelope

6.

1.

viruses

host cell nucleus

5. New viruses are put together inside host cell.

5.

4.

HOST CELL

2.

4. Host cell makes copies of viral DNA.

3.

2. Viruses enter host cell.

3. Genetic material from viruses moves into host cell.

genetic material

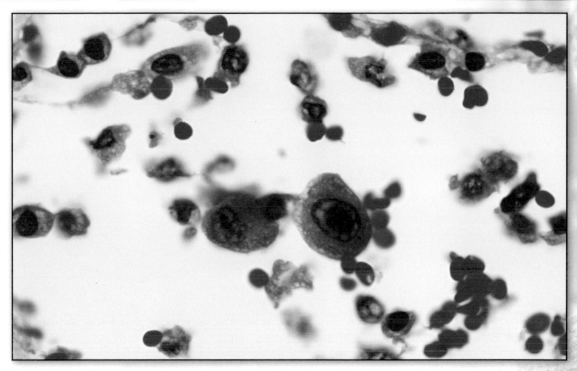

Some viruses, such as HIV, weaken the body's immune (defense) system. That allows other disease organisms to invade easily. The black dots on this section through a human lung are *Pneumocystis carinii* fungi, which cause a form of pneumonia. Pneumonia is common in people with AIDS, which is caused by HIV.

surface of a suitable cell, their next problem is how to get into it. Different viruses use different strategies. Some viruses have outer membranes that fuse with the host cell membrane and then release the viral capsid into the cell. In other cases only the viral DNA or RNA enters the cell.

In most cases the viral genes soon get to work to create more viruses. Viruses use their host cell's chemical machinery to start making viral enzymes and the coat proteins that are needed for new viral capsids. At the same time, the viral genes make new copies of themselves.

VIRAL INFECTIONS THROUGH HISTORY

Viruses have always caused diseases in people. One of the earliest records of a viral infection is a 3,500-year-old Egyptian carving showing a priest with a shriveled leg—a classic sign of polio. Some viruses, such as those causing influenza, have been known for thousands of years. Others, such as HIV, have appeared much more recently.

When these various tasks have been completed, the capsids and the viral genes come together and assemble into new viruses. Depending on the type of virus involved, this action may take place in the cell's nucleus (control center) or in its cytoplasm, the fluid flowing around inside the cell. The new viruses may then bud out of the host cell's membrane, or the whole cell may weaken and burst to release the viruses.

Sometimes, while viral reproduction takes place, there is a struggle for control between the virus and cell. Some cells are programmed to self-destruct if attacked by a virus, for example, but there are certain viruses so well adapted that they can switch off this program.

Some viruses produce latent infection of a host—the viral genes remain inactive between the time of infection

The distortion in the tulip shown here was caused by a viral infection common to certain varieties of tulip.

BACULOVIRUSES

The baculoviruses are a virus family that attacks only insects. Baculoviruses therefore have potential for controlling insect pests. The insects die after eating plants contaminated with the viruses. In the United States baculoviruses are already used successfully against pests, especially caterpillars such as the cotton bollworm, corn earworm, and the young of gypsy moths.

and the appearance of symptoms. The herpesvirus that causes cold sores, for example, can go through many cycles of active infection and latency. Not all viruses immediately start to make new copies of themselves when they enter a host cell. Some viruses, such as the human immunodeficiency virus (HIV), which causes AIDS, combine their genes with the host cell's DNA. This action helps the viruses hide from attack by the host's immune (defense) systems or by drugs.

VIRUSES AND PLANTS

Plant viruses, which can cause major damage to agricultural crops, are commonly spread by sap-sucking insects. It is not possible or practical to vaccinate plants, or give them a substance to prevent disease. So most control efforts center on trying to kill the insects that spread the disease. Plants can be bred to be genetically resistant to particular viruses. The first virus to be discovered, in 1892, was a plant virus called tobacco mosaic virus, or TMV. Many discoveries about the structure and molecular biology of viruses were made by scientists studying TMV.

VIRUSES AND ILLNESS

Diseases caused by viruses range from the nuisance of the common cold to serious and sometimes fatal infections such as rabies. Although they come in a bewildering variety, viral diseases show some underlying patterns that can help us understand viral behavior.

Disease-causing viruses need to find cells in which to reproduce. These cells tend to be the ones that are easily gotten to. The living cells that line your breathing

The common cold is a viral infection of the nose and throat. It causes a sore throat, runny nose, sneezing, and sometimes a fever. There is no cure for a cold. The best way of fighting the disease is to try to stop the virus from being spread: by washing hands, using disinfectants, and keeping away from infected people. The cold virus is often spread by spray from sneezing people.

A typical measles rash on the back of a patient. The measles virus first infects the lungs and then spreads through the bloodstream to infect other parts of the body. It can cause a very serious fever (extremely high body temperature).

system and gut are obvious targets. Many viruses, such as those that cause influenza, are adapted to infect the lungs and throat, and are spread through droplets in the air.

Other viruses, including the poliomyelitis virus (poliovirus), live in the wall of the gut after first being swallowed. Some, such as the yellow fever virus, rely on bloodsucking insects to carry them from one person to another.

The poliovirus is an important example of how viruses can cause different effects in different parts of the body. Usually it lives harmlessly in the gut; but if it spreads into the nervous system, it can cause paralysis and death. Before a

suitable vaccine—a substance that prevents disease—was developed against polio in the mid-20th century, the disease was a greatly feared killer, especially of children.

Many viruses such as measles cause a single, limited infection, after which the victim usually recovers and is then protected against the virus for life. Others, particularly the herpesviruses, do not disappear but become latent, hiding within nerve cells without causing any visible symptoms. They may then reactivate years later. For example, the herpesvirus that causes chicken pox can reemerge later as shingles, a painful disease of the nerves and skin. Yet other viruses such as HIV never become

HIV AND AIDS

After the AIDS epidemic began in the United States around 1980, researchers worked frantically to discover its cause. In 1983 they succeeded in identifying the culprit—a virus now called human immunodeficiency virus, or HIV. HIV attacks the body's immune (defense) system. An infected person cannot fight off the infections that healthy people normally can. As it grows and multiplies, HIV also constantly changes its protein coat, making the search for an effective vaccine much more difficult.

Blood is tested for antibodies produced to fight the HIV infection; the virus is not tested for directly.

latent but continue to reproduce and may eventually overwhelm their victim. Some viruses make their host cells divide in an uncontrolled way, causing cancer.

Some viruses, including smallpox and measles, only cause infection in humans. Others, notably rabies, can infect almost all vertebrates (animals with backbones). Viruses caught from other animals can be the most dangerous because they are not in balance with the human body and may kill quickly, even if the virus itself is also killed in the process. An example is the Ebola virus of tropical Africa, which originates in monkeys and apes. It can cause fatal bleeding if it infects people.

Some effects of viruses are indirect. Influenza (flu), for example, can weaken people so they catch potentially fatal bacterial infections. Similarly, HIV damages the immune system, allowing other infections to take hold in the body.

HEPATITIS

The three viruses hepatitis A, B, and C cause diseases in humans. With names like that, you might expect them to be related to each other, but they are not. Hepatitis A is in the same family as the poliovirus, while hepatitis C is related to the yellow fever virus. Hepatitis B belongs to yet another family of viruses. However, they all cause hepatitis—inflammation of the liver—and are dangerous. Hepatitis C has the added danger that no vaccine has yet been developed against it.

A woman gets a flu vaccination.

Many, although not all, viral diseases can now be prevented by vaccination, usually by injecting a vaccine made of an inactive virus or viral parts. However, there are still relatively few effective drugs to treat viruses once a person is infected. Viruses grow only inside cells, and so culturing viruses (growing them in a laboratory) means culturing cells, too. This procedure is relatively easy for most bacteria or plants, but getting animal cells to grow in a lab is much more difficult. Some important viruses, such as hepatitis C, still cannot be grown in tissue culture. That makes it much more difficult for scientists to produce vaccines against them.

THE EFFECT OF VIRUSES ON THE ENVIRONMENT

Viruses are usually thought of in terms of the damage they cause—to people, livestock, or crop plants. However, viruses are also a part of Earth's natural ecology. Scientists are just beginning to find out how viruses fit into the working of natural ecosystems.

WHAT ARE PRIONS?

In recent years scientists have discovered a new class of disease-causing agents called prions. They are not viruses because they do not contain DNA or RNA. Instead, they are simply a particular type of protein, similar to a normal protein found in the human body, that somehow causes the body to make more prion copies. Many scientists think prions cause so-called mad cow disease and its human equivalent, Creutzfeldt-Jakob disease (CJD, or new-variant CJD). Both are fatal diseases in which the brain gradually degenerates (breaks down).

FOOD FOR VIRUSES

The first evidence that some viruses could attack bacteria came in 1915. They were named bacteriophages (which means "bacteria eaters"), or phages (right). Bacteria are relatively easy to grow in culture, and thus much of the basic knowledge about how viruses work has come from studying phages. The larger phages have a complex structure that allows them to inject their DNA into their victims. Scientists made history in 1975 when for the first time they figured out the complete genome (the total genetic makeup) of a natural life form, a small RNA bacteriophage called phiX174. Although the methods they used were very time consuming by today's standards, the scientists' achievement helped others figure out the human genome and the genomes of other large organisms.

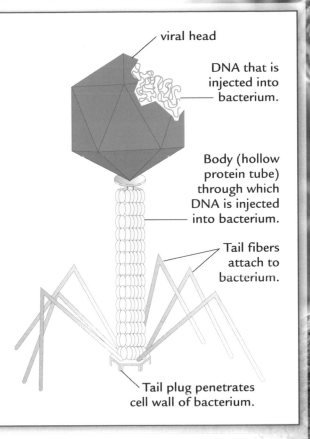

viral head

DNA that is injected into bacterium.

Body (hollow protein tube) through which DNA is injected into bacterium.

Tail fibers attach to bacterium.

Tail plug penetrates cell wall of bacterium.

Lakes and oceans are good places in which viruses can survive. There can be 10 billion or more bacteria-eating viruses in 2 pints (1 liter) of seawater. Generally viruses have a major effect on bacteria populations and therefore on natural cycles such as the carbon cycle. Some protists may even be able to trap and digest viruses, so viruses may form an important part of the food chain.

WHAT ARE COMPUTER VIRUSES?

When computer scientists first began to use the term *virus* when referring to nuisance pieces of software, they hit on a very intelligent comparison. Just like real viruses, computer viruses can take over a host, disrupt its workings, and cause it to make more copies of the virus. People now even use words that relate to ecology to talk about computer viruses. In farming, monoculture means growing the same crops over a wide area, so if disease appears, all the crops are vulnerable since they all have similar genes. In computers, monoculture occurs when most people are using the same operating system or software. Computer viruses built to attack these systems therefore spread quickly.

CHAPTER FIVE

THE CONNECTION BETWEEN MICROORGANISMS AND DISEASE

Most of the billions of dollars that are spent on the study of microorganisms worldwide are aimed toward combating diseases.

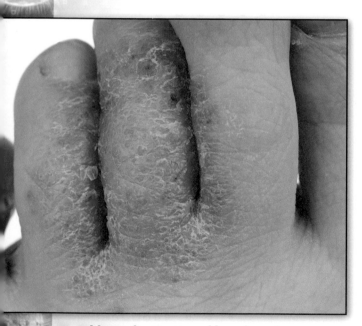

Athlete's foot is caused by a fungal infection of skin between the toes. The condition is sometimes also called ringworm of the feet.

An infectious disease is one you can catch from another person or sometimes from an animal. Not all diseases are infectious; some are caused by faulty genes and others by a poor diet or habits such as cigarette smoking.

Bacteria and viruses cause many of the world's infectious diseases, although some illnesses, such as malaria, are caused by protists. The long list of human illnesses caused by bacteria includes major killers such as plague, diphtheria, typhoid, syphilis, tuberculosis, cholera, and anthrax. Many other serious diseases are caused by viruses and include smallpox, AIDS (acquired immune deficiency syndrome), and influenza. Microscopic fungi can cause a number of human diseases, ranging from athlete's foot to serious lung infections. Such fungi are also a major cause of disease in plants.

WHAT ARE PATHOGENS?

Microorganisms that cause disease are called pathogens (literally "disease

DISEASE TRANSMISSION

Many species of bacteria and viruses rely on hitching a ride in water droplets that are coughed or sneezed out by an infected person and then breathed in by someone else. Other microorganisms are carried in food or drink, which is then said to be contaminated. These diseases attack the body via the gut. Others can be caught by touching a person's skin or coming into contact with their body fluids. Yet others rely on being transported by bloodsucking insects, such as mosquitoes, while some are spread accidentally by needles used for injection. Some infections, including AIDS, can be passed on from a mother to her unborn child in the uterus.

producers"). Some potential pathogens, such as the bacterium that causes tetanus (lockjaw), usually live harmlessly in the soil. However, they cause infection if they get into deep wounds.

Pathogens vary a great deal in how easily they are transmitted and in the particular way they enter the body (see above). They also differ in how well they can survive in the outside environment. Some pathogens, such as those causing smallpox and syphilis, cannot survive outside the human body. The virus that causes hoof-and-mouth disease in cattle, by contrast, can

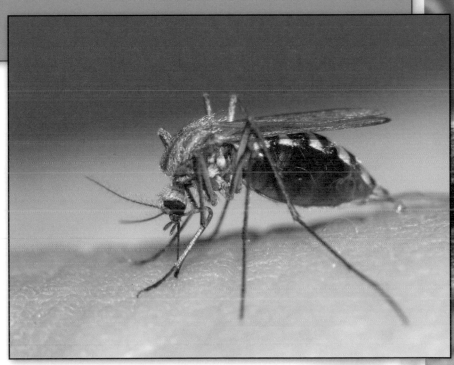

A mosquito feeds on human blood. Mosquitoes spread diseases such as malaria, which is caused by *Plasmodium* parasites. The parasites are injected into the body as the mosquito feeds. They multiply in the blood and the liver, causing fevers and chills. Malaria can kill a person.

be blown for miles in the wind and still be infectious. Some bacteria (notably the anthrax bacterium) form long-lasting structures called spores, which can contaminate soil for years.

A sign in the UK warns people to keep out of this farmland in order to prevent the spread of foot-and-mouth (also known as hoof-and-mouth) disease.

HOW DISEASE IS SPREAD

Some diseases lead to epidemics; that is, they can sweep through a whole community, often very quickly. Understanding the pattern of a particular disease is important for controlling and coping with it. For example, ordinary life for AIDS sufferers became a little easier once people understood that they could not catch the virus by casual contact, such as by shaking hands. The virus that causes AIDS is spread by bodily fluids, that is, through contaminated blood in syringes or transfusions or through sexual contact.

Cholera is an example of a disease that is not normally caught directly from another person but almost always from contaminated water or food. Certain diseases such as typhoid have the added problem that some people are carriers. Carriers have the bacterium but do not get ill, although they pass the illness to others. Other diseases, including anthrax, move only among animals, not people.

The symptoms of diseases take different amounts of time to show after the infection reaches the body. That time is called the incubation period. It can be a few days, weeks, or even months. With diseases such as AIDS or syphilis, the full-blown disease can take years to develop. Pathogens often cause different problems depending

WHAT ARE PANDEMICS?

A pandemic is an epidemic on a grand scale, such as one that sweeps across a continent or even spreads throughout the world. A famous example is the Black Death. This outbreak of plague swept across Europe between 1346 and 1350, killing up to one-third of the total population. Another example is the deadly strain of influenza called Spanish flu, which appeared in 1918, just before the end of World War I (1914–1918). It killed 20 million people, more than were killed in the war itself.

This is a zebu cow. Zebu are the only cows that can be kept over much of Africa. They are more resistant to nagana, a disease spread by tsetse flies, than other cattle. However, even zebu cannot be kept in many forested African regions.

on where they spread to in the body. A general disease category such as pneumonia (inflammation of the lungs) can result from infection by many different pathogens.

FIGHTING DISEASE

The human body is not defenseless against invading microorganisms.

Millions of years of evolution mean that we have inherited many ways of excluding or attacking potential dangers to the body. We are now also able to alert the body in advance artificially, through the process of immunization.

The skin, with its thick outer layer of dead cells, is a good barrier to infection. Other surfaces, such as the lining of the gut and air passages, consist of living cells and are more vulnerable (open to attack). However, these surfaces are protected by sticky mucus that helps prevent

KOCH AND PASTEUR

The researches of Louis Pasteur and Robert Koch showed that infectious diseases were caused by microorganisms. For a long time people had suspected that this is what happened, but there were alternative ideas that confused the issue. One popular idea was that these types of diseases were caused by contaminated or bad air and not by anything living. The mistaken idea that decaying matter could give rise to entirely new life by spontaneous generation was also a source of confusion.

DISEASE OPPORTUNISTS

Diseases are often made more complicated by other microorganisms that arrive after the first one has infected. They are called secondary infections. For example, the influenza virus can kill people in frail health by weakening them so much that bacterial infections take hold. In AIDS the immune (defense) system itself is greatly weakened. That makes it possible for a variety of microorganisms to infect the body when they would otherwise be easily dealt with and repelled.

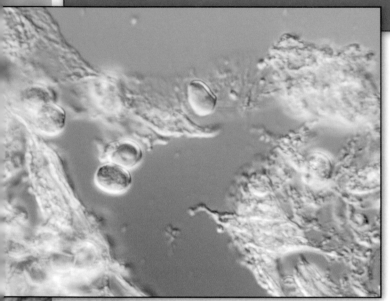

Pneumocystic carinii **spores are shown here growing in the lung of an AIDS patient. This parasite is responsible for one of the most common infections among AIDS patients.**

microorganisms from reaching the cells. Human cells also secrete chemicals that are poisonous to many bacteria. Harmless bacteria grow in the mouth linings and elsewhere, making it more difficult for the dangerous species to get a hold.

Other defenders against foreign invaders are phagocytes—wandering amebalike cells that swallow particles they come across. Infectious diseases can cause an inflammatory response, in which the affected area becomes hot, swollen, and painful. Sometimes the overall body temperature rises, and there is a fever. Whether fever helps the body is not always clear, although some microorganisms are

DEADLY BY-PRODUCTS

Sometimes bacteria cause illness and death not because they infect vital organs directly but because they produce deadly toxins (poisons). The bacteria that cause diphtheria, a serious disease that makes the throat swell, do not spread beyond the throat, but they produce one of the most deadly toxins known. The toxin causes inflammation of the heart and nervous system. Toxins may help bacteria repel body cells that are attacking them and damage cells to allow the bacteria to feed on them.

A child is immunized against polio in Jakarta, Indonesia. Amid fears that the disease would spread, Indonesia began a nationwide vaccination campaign, targeting 24 million children under the age of 5.

inactivated by higher temperatures. Many other symptoms such as spots on the skin can be caused by the body's own reactions to infection rather than by the pathogen itself.

If any pathogens manage to get past these various defenses, there is a sophisticated response called the induced immune response. In it the body produces antibodies, which are protein molecules tailored to fit onto a particular type of invading microorganism. The antibodies may float in the body fluids or be attached to cells. Antibodies help in the identification and destruction of invaders.

The first time a particular organism invades, it may take time for the body to produce antibodies against it. After the infection is over, the body usually keeps a stock of so-called memory cells. They can produce antibodies again quickly if there is ever a second attack. This mechanism provides a lifelong protection against many diseases.

THE HISTORY OF IMMUNIZATION

Immunization started long before people knew about the immune system or micro-organisms. In ancient China, and later in Europe, material from smallpox patients was used to immunize (inoculate) other people against smallpox—a very risky procedure. In 1798 the English physician Edward Jenner (1749–1823) proved that a milder disease, cow-pox, protected against smallpox. This procedure was later called vaccination (from the Latin *vacca*, meaning "cow"). Smallpox vaccination was the only type available until 1885, when French scientist Louis Pasteur (1822–1895) introduced a vaccine against rabies (a viral disease of the nervous system). Many other vaccines have been developed.

English physician Edward Jenner is shown here vaccinating a small child against smallpox using cowpox serum. His efforts led to almost complete eradication of the virus.

VACCINATING AGAINST DISEASE

In modern times physicians have found out how to put the natural body system on alert artificially using vaccines. Vaccines are preparations that resemble an invading organism (pathogen) but are not dangerous. They are either live but harmless versions of the pathogen or are killed pathogens (or parts of them). Anything that gets the immune system to produce suitable antibodies and does not have dangerous side-efffects is a potential vaccine.

It can be very hard to develop and test a new vaccine. It took almost 40 years for a polio vaccine to be developed, for example. Some important patho-gens, such as HIV (the cause of AIDS) and hepatitis C virus, still lack vaccines against them, greatly hindering the fight against these diseases. Other pathogens, including those that cause influenza and sleeping sickness, can change their prop-erties quickly, so a vaccine is no longer effective against them.

A major success for public health came in the 1970s, when naturally occur-ring smallpox was finally wiped out in the

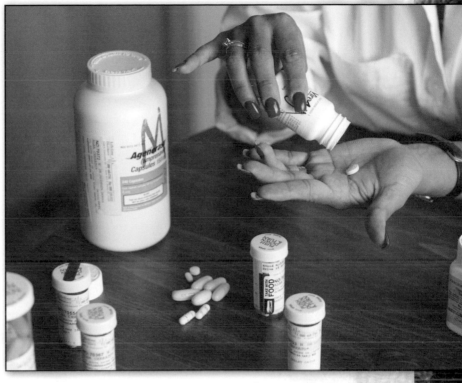

A patient prepares to take her cocktail of 14 different AIDS medications that she takes three times daily. There is no vaccine against HIV, but sufferers can stay healthy with the help of medication.

world after a huge vaccination campaign. The last known case was in Somalia, Africa, in 1977. Smallpox was easier to wipe out because it infects only humans, and because its vaccine is also a live virus. People can catch the vaccine virus from each other without even knowing it. If smallpox ever reappears, it will only be through accidental or deliberate release of the smallpox virus, now kept securely in laboratories.

TREATMENT OF DISEASE

There are two main ways to tackle infectious disease. First, physicians can focus on preventing and treating disease in individual sufferers. Second, society as a whole can try and minimize the risk of disease in a particular area or even wipe it out altogether.

To treat an illness properly, physicians need to know what it is. Diagnosing an infectious disease is not always easy. For example, many infections cause similar fevers, and by the time it is obvious

THE COST OF MEDICINE

In many poorer countries of the world people cannot afford expensive drugs to treat diseases such as AIDS. They say that drugs should be made cheaper in such countries. Drug companies have sometimes permitted this, but the firms also point out that they have invested huge amounts of money in developing drugs, and they must be able to get it back to keep their business going. How do you think drugs should be priced, and who should pay for them?

Fred Soper (1893–1975) was famous for preventive medicine and public health. He worked on the eradication of hookworm, malaria, yellow fever, and typhus in tropical areas.

what the disease is, it may be too late to treat it. Modern science has made it easier to identify which agent is causing a disease. Numerous laboratory tests, often based on specific reactions with antibodies, are now available to identify which type of pathogen is responsible for a disease.

Before the 20th century many people died unnecessarily in hospitals because doctors did not realize the importance of cleanliness in preventing infection. When the role of bacteria in disease was recognized in the 1860s, pioneers such as the English surgeon Joseph Lister (1827–1912) started to clean their instruments using antiseptics in operating rooms. That greatly reduced the risk of later infection. Antiseptics are substances that check the growth of microorganisms.

PREVENTING AN OUTBREAK

In the wider community public health measures such as preventing water supplies from being contaminated by sewage helped stop the spread of typhoid and cholera. These

MALARIA PREVENTION

Malaria is diagnosed by finding the parasites that cause it in stained blood smears examined under a microscope. Effective synthetic drugs destroy the malarial parasites inside red blood cells. At first these drugs relieved symptoms of an attack that had already started, prevented attacks, and even wiped out the infection. By the late 20th century, however, some strains had become resistant to the drugs, so the incidence of malaria began to increase after a steady decline.

The basic method of prevention is to eliminate the breeding places of carrier *Anopheles* mosquitoes by draining and filling marshes, swamps, stagnant pools, and other standing water. Some insecticides can be used to control mosquitoes. Window screens and mosquito netting are used as physical barriers too. Natural resistance and acquired immunity through previous exposure reduce susceptibility to malaria.

and many other pathogens are common in the environment. People can prevent disease simply by avoiding contact with the microorganisms through using clean water.

Tuberculosis (TB) is a major killer. The disease is passed between people and caught from milk from infected cows. Improved housing, pasteurization of milk, and eradication of the disease in cattle have helped reduce TB infection in Europe and North America to low levels. Routine vaccination of people is also important in preventing this and many other diseases.

Identifying the source of a disease outbreak is important, whether it is a food source that is contaminated

or, as with Legionnaire's disease, an air-conditioning system that harbors a serious lung illness.

The cinchona tree is a source of quinine. Quinine is extracted from the dried bark and used to treat the deadly disease malaria.

HOW ANTIBIOTICS WORK

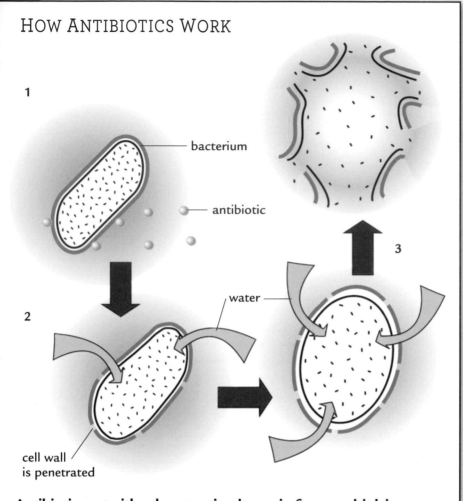

Antibiotics act either by stopping bacteria from multiplying or by killing them. Antibiotics kill bacteria by breaking down their cell walls (1). As a result, water enters the bacterium (2). Eventually so much water enters that the bacterium bursts (3).

healthcare workers can replace the fluid and salts, the sufferer usually recovers.

Drugs are also important weapons against invading microorganisms. Some drugs have been used for hundreds of years. For example, quinine, obtained from the bark of a South American tree, is effective against malaria. Other early drugs such as mercury compounds were sometimes effective, but they had dangerous side effects. Ideally, a drug should hit the pathogen without damaging the body at the same time.

A great step forward came in the 20th century with the discovery of antibiotics (meaning "'anti-life"). These substances attack bacteria; they are produced by microorganisms such as molds. There are probably millions of different antibiotics produced in nature, but only a small fraction are suitable to inject safely into humans. Many synthetic antibiotics are also now made.

Sometimes simple treatment methods can make a big difference in the fight against diseases. With cholera, for example, the main symptom is severe diarrhea. Untreated cholera victims, often children, usually die by losing too much water and too many body salts. If

RESISTANCE TO ANTIBIOTICS

In most countries antibiotics are available only by prescription from a physician—you cannot buy them over the counter. That is because the more antibiotics are used unnecessarily, the more likely bacteria are to become resistant to them. Bacteria reproduce very quickly. Sometimes mistakes during reproduction cause mutations that might allow a bacterium to resist the effects of antibiotics. This beneficial mutation soon spreads as bacteria continue to reproduce quickly. The bacteria are then said to have developed antibiotic resistance. What makes this situation worse is that genes that build resistance to antibiotics are often carried on small, separate pieces of DNA, called plasmids. Plasmids can be transferred between different types of bacteria. Thus antibiotic resistance spreads easily and is a growing problem.

Antibiotics are usually very specific in their actions. For example, some antibiotics interfere with the bacteria's cell wall (see left). Different antibiotics work best against different organisms. Penicillin, for example, is ineffective against the plague bacterium, although several other antibiotics do work.

THE TREATMENT OF VIRUSES

Drugs that attack viruses are called antivirals. Some of them work by interfering with how the virus copies its genes, others by knocking out enzymes produced by the virus. Few effective antiviral drugs have been discovered so far. This situation is particularly serious for viral diseases for which there is no vaccine, such as HIV. There are some success stories, however. For example, HIV sufferers can now be given a combination of several different antivirals that help keep the virus in their body under control. An antiviral called acyclovir is now widely used to control and reduce infections caused by herpesviruses.

THE INFLUENCE OF KOCH

In 1880 the German physician Robert Koch (1843–1910) was the first person to prove that an infectious disease (anthrax) was caused by a bacterium. He developed several principles, now called Koch's postulates, to guide other researchers. The aim was to confirm if a particular pathogen caused a certain disease. Koch said that a suspected pathogen should be grown in a pure culture, and that this culture should be shown to cause the disease in unaffected individuals. However, Koch's postulates cannot always be followed; there are some viruses and bacteria that cannot yet be successfully grown in culture.

CHAPTER SIX

USEFUL MICROORGANISMS

Lactic acid bacteria, like the ones shown in color here, are used in yogurt making. Some nutrition experts promote eating yogurt because the good bacteria in yogurt help with digestion.

Microorganisms are vital in many industries, such as food and drink manufacture, biotechnology, and waste management.

People tend to associate microorganisms only with infections and diseases. Most microorganisms, however, are harmless to humans. Many are even helpful to us. Bacteria inside our intestines help us digest food, for example, while those on our skin help the body fight off disease-causing bacteria.

As early as 4,000 years ago the Egyptians used a single-celled fungus called yeast to help make bread and wine. They did not realize that tiny creatures, too small to see, were essential to produce these foods. Microorganisms and their biological processes are now used widely in the food industry, in medicine, in pest control, in the treatment of wastes and pollution, and in the creation of new products. In addition, the expanding revolution in genetic engineering would be impossible without

Fermented soybean curd (a kind of tofu) is a popular condiment in China. Asian people have made and eaten bean curds for many centuries. They are a low-fat source of protein, calcium, and iron. Dried soybeans are soaked in water, then crushed and boiled. The resulting soy milk is separated from the solids, or curds. The curd is poured into molds and cut into squares.

microorganisms. These applications are examples of biotechnology, which is the commercial, industrial, and technical use of biological knowledge.

MICROORGANISMS AND FOOD

Most of the foods people make using microorganisms are produced by fermentation. Fermentation is carried out by anaerobic microorganisms, which are able to live without the gas oxygen (*anaerobic* means "oxygen hating"). They include types of bacteria, yeasts (single-celled fungi), and molds. Fermentation generally involves breaking sugars down into simpler substances. There are different types of fermentation that produce a range of by-products with distinctive and pleasant tastes.

Common fermented foods include cheese, yogurt, salami, bread, pickles, sauerkraut, olives, and tofu. They have different properties and taste very different from their starting materials. Fermentation by-products are often acids or alcohols (such as ethanol). Acids and alcohols preserve food by killing food-spoiling microorganisms.

Another product of fermentation is mycoprotein, a chewy, protein-rich food made by a fungus. This cheap alternative to meat is made in large fermentation towers. Industrial or farm waste is used to feed the fungus. Mycoprotein is textured and flavored to resemble meat. It is a good source of fiber, protein, vitamin B, iron, and zinc.

ENZYME ACTION

Anerobic microorganisms contain enzymes that enable them to ferment foods. Enzymes are proteins that speed up chemical reactions. Scientists can remove some enzymes from

BREWING BEER WITH YEAST

Beer brewers need four ingredients: barley, hops, water, and yeast. First, the barley is soaked in water to soften the grain and allowed to germinate, or sprout. This process is called malting: It encourages natural enzymes in the barley to change long starch molecules into short sugar molecules (glucose). The sugars can be fermented by the yeast. The glucose solution is poured into large fermentation tanks containing yeast. The mixture is kept warm and free of oxygen.

In a few weeks the yeast turns glucose into ethanol and carbon dioxide gas. They give the beer its alcohol content and its carbonation, or fizziness. Hops are added for bitterness and aroma.

Fermentation tanks in a brewery. The tanks contain yeast, which turns sugars into alcohol and fizzy carbon dioxide gas.

Microorganisms turn sugar in pickled (part-fermented) vegetables into weak acids.

microorganisms for use in industry. In the baking industry enzymes made by fungi and bacteria are added to flour to improve the quality of bread, cookies, and crackers.

Enzymes from microorganisms are used in the production of juices, wine, carbonated drinks, cheese, syrups, coffee, salad dressings, and meat tenderizers. They are also used extensively

CHEESEMAKING

People use bacteria to make fermented dairy products such as cheese. The bacteria change the milk sugar lactose into lactic acid. Various mixtures of the bacteria *Streptococcus* and *Lactobacillus*, called starter cultures, are used to ferment the solid portion of curdled (partly soured) milk—the curds. A wide variety of flavors and textures can be obtained by varying the starter cultures, temperatures, and conditions or by adding microorganisms. Different fungi can be added to make blue cheese, camembert, or brie, for example.

WHAT ARE PLASMIDS?

Plasmids are small loops of DNA that occur naturally in many types of bacteria. Bacteria often swap plasmid DNA between themselves. Enzymes called restriction enzymes cut the plasmid ring. Another enzyme, DNA ligase, inserts a new section of DNA and links up the plasmid ring. Scientists have taken advantage of the DNA-swapping properties of bacterial plasmids in genetic engineering technology.

Plasmids are small and easy to handle. They can be extracted from one cell and inserted into another. So geneticists can use plasmids to introduce foreign DNA into cells. Plasmids used in this way are called plasmid vectors (carriers). Plasmid vectors allow scientists to introduce genes with useful properties, such as producing a chemical that is used as a drug, into other bacteria. Geneticists also add antibiotic-resistance genes that will help them sort out the successfully engineered bacteria at the end of the process. One resistance gene is linked to the useful DNA; the other is not.

In the genetic engineering process plasmids from bacteria (1) are cut using a restriction enzyme (2). A foreign DNA fragment is introduced, and the DNA ligase is added (3). Some plasmids re-form as they were; others incorporate the foreign DNA and the

in nonfood industries, such as laundry and dry-cleaning processes, textiles and paper making, and in medicine.

People have genetically engineered microorganisms that can make useful enzymes.

GM FOOD AND ANTIBIOTICS

Genetically modified (GM) crops often contain marker genes. They are inserted into crops along with other genes that produce the desired characteristic, such as resistance to frost damage. Marker genes show whether or not the new, useful gene has been successfully inserted. Marker genes are generally bacterial genes. They might also produce resistance to certain antibiotics. People are increasingly worried about whether antibiotic-resistant genes can be passed from crops to disease-causing bacteria in the human gut. That might make pathogens immune to antibiotics.

CREATING A SUPERBUG

Genetic engineers are designing a bacterium that can break down radioactive wastes. In the 1950s scientists discovered a bacterium that can survive 1,000 times more radiation than a person. High levels of radiation damage a cell's DNA, but these bacteria can repair their damaged DNA within 12 to 24 hours. Researchers want to alter the bacteria by adding genes from another type of bacteria that can break down the toxic chemicals often mixed with radioactive wastes in underground tanks. They hope to create bacteria that can break down these chemicals while surviving high levels of radiation.

antibiotics. The mixture is inserted into a new set of bacterial cells (4). Some bacteria do not take up the plasmid, others incorporate unaltered plasmids. A small proportion will now contain the useful plasmid. To separate the mixture, the geneticist grows the bacteria on a gel containing antibiotic A. Only bacteria that contain the plasmid with the gene for antibiotic A resistance (and, therefore, the linked useful gene) will grow (5). To double-check their results, scientists add bacteria to a dish that contains both antibiotics (6). Bacteria that grew on the first dish but not on the second have taken up the useful DNA.

PLASMID VECTOR

antibiotic B resistance gene

antibiotic A resistance gene

restriction enzyme cut site

GENETIC ENGINEERING WITH PLASMIDS

1 bacteria containing plasmids — plasmid

2 restriction enzyme

3 recombinant DNA

4 foreign DNA — bacterium containing recombinant DNA

5 Only bacteria with recombinant DNA survive.

Antibiotic A

6 Only bacteria without any recombinant DNA survive.

Antibiotics A and B

MICROORGANISMS AND GENETIC ENGINEERING

Microorganisms play a vital role in the field of genetic engineering. Genetic engineers take genes from different sources and recombine them to produce new types of plants, animals, or microorganisms with useful features. Microorganisms are the tools genetic engineers use to modify and move deoxyribonucleic acid (DNA) from one organism to another. DNA carries an

20TH-CENTURY PESTICIDE

In 1916 the Japanese beetle was accidentally introduced to the eastern United States. By the 1930s it had seriously infested crops (see right). Biologists searched frantically for natural enemies capable of stopping the hungry bug. Finally, they discovered a sick beetle larva (grub) and figured out that its disease was caused by a spore-forming bacterium. In a process that is still used now, scientists crushed and dried infected beetle larvae and sprinkled them over crops. The powder containing spores of the bacteria was eaten by the larvae, which then became infected and died.

organism's genes. A human-made DNA molecule that contains genes from different sources is called recombinant DNA.

Bacteria are particularly useful to genetic engineers. Some bacterial enzymes can act as either scissors or glue. Geneticists use such enzymes to cut up DNA or patch together recombinant DNA.

Bacteria also contain rings of DNA called plasmids. Plasmids can carry genes into crops or other organisms. Genetic engineers sometimes prefer to use bacteriophages, which are viruses that attack only bacteria. Bacteriophages can insert DNA into bacteria.

THE PROS AND CONS OF GENETICALLY MODIFIED (GM) CROPS

GM food enables farmers to increase their yields (harvests) and use less herbicides (weed killers) and pesticides (pest killers). But there may be side effects to growing and eating GM crops.

Arguments for
• Harvests are bigger.
• Crop losses from pests, weeds, and diseases can be reduced.
• Pesticide and herbicide use can be lessened in some cases.
• Crops can be designed with useful features, such as glowing to show ill health.
• The growing world population needs tougher crops that can grow in places previously unsuitable for farming.

Arguments against
• May pass genes for pesticide resistance to pests and genes for herbicide resistance to weeds.
• More likely to cause allergic reactions in people.
• The seeds of patented (legally protected) GM crops can be expensive to buy.
• Human disease-causing bacteria may become resistant to antibiotics (antibiotic-resistant genes are used in markers in GM crops).

A group of campaigners against genetically modified food protest at a farm where oilseed rape crops are growing.

BT CROPS AND ORGANIC FARMING

Organic farmers, who do not use artificial fertilizers and pesticides, have sprayed their crops with the bacterium *Bacillus thuringiensis* (Bt) since the early 1960s. It was discovered then that these bacteria produce toxins that kill agricultural pests without harming other animals. Since the 1990s some biotechnology companies have genetically modified strains of Bt and inserted Bt genes directly into crops to give built-in pest protection. Some people oppose the use of Bt crops because they might make pests resistant to Bt toxins. That would make Bt toxin useless for organic farming.

The use of genetically modified organisms (GMOs) has exploded in the last 20 years. This has led to growing arguments over their release into the environment. Much disagreement about genetically engineered products centers around genetically modified (GM) foods. Increasingly GMOs are replacing the microorganisms that have previously been used to make food products, and scientists commonly put bacterial genes into crops.

The most common crops that contain bacterial genes are corn, soybeans, canola, and cotton. They are engineered to be resistant to pests and herbicides (weed killers). The toxin (poison) produced by a bacterium called *Bacillus thuringiensis* (Bt) has been used most often in GM crops to kill pests. While

These genetically modified soybeans were developed to provide high-protein animal feed. GM crops are developed by scientists using bacteria or viruses to engineer new DNA.

BACTERIA AND POLLUTANTS

Researchers have genetically engineered a new bacterium to detect herbicide pollution in the environment. It contains a firefly gene that makes the cell glow when it detects certain herbicides and other pollutants. Similar methods are being developed to create microorganisms that detect explosives or biological weapons.

BIOTERRORISM

Disease-causing bacteria, such as those that cause plague, anthrax, and tularemia, could be used by terrorists who could spray them over a city or release them into the water supply to kill people. The bioterrorism debate focuses on what to do in the event of an attack. How do we prevent the spread of diseases and treat infected people?

GM foods can help farmers raise more crops with lower costs, some people believe that growing and eating these crops may have unexpected side effects.

WASTE CLEANUP

As the world population grows, more and more industrial pollutants and wastes are

BACTERIA AND OIL SPILLS

In 1989 the Exxon tanker *Valdez* ran aground near Prince William Sound, Alaska, spilling millions of gallons of oil into the water and coating almost 1,200 miles (1,900km) of coastline. Microbiologists soon found naturally occurring bacteria that could break down, or biodegrade, oil. But laboratory tests showed that bacterial growth was limited by the amounts of nitrogen and phosphorus present in the seawater. These nutrients are present in fertilizers. Spraying a solution of fertilizers onto patches of contaminated beach showed dramatic effects after only 10 days. Using the fertilizer sped up oil biodegradation from the predicted 10 to 20 years to just 2 to 3 years.

Crews work to clean up oil washed ashore at Pensacola Beach in Florida. Bacteria that can naturally break down oil are often used in cleanups like this one.

being produced, many of them highly poisonous. Most pollutants are burned, buried, or treated with chemicals. But many end up in our air, water, or soil. In the last 30 years scientists have found biological methods of treating wastes and cleaning up polluted sites. They use microorganisms such as bacteria to break down pollutants and turn them into less poisonous substances. Most people think that these methods of waste and pollution control are more environmentally friendly and cheaper than the usual methods. The cleanup of pollutants using microorganisms is called bioremediation.

A single teaspoon of soil contains at least 100 million microorganisms. Most break down organic material such as dead plants and animals. Some of these microorganisms gain energy by breaking down particular pollutants. The job of a microbiologist working on a bioremediation project is to find and encourage the growth of certain microorganisms that break down a targeted pollutant.

To make sure the microorganisms are able to destroy the pollutants, a microbiologist must figure out their basic needs. All organisms need water, food, and a source of energy. Different types of microorganisms need different types of foods and environments to grow properly. Some need oxygen, while others do not. Some like high temperatures, but many die if the temperature increases too much. Microorganisms are also affected by the availability of nutrients, the pH (level of acidity), the amount of pollutant, and how poisonous the pollutant is.

One of the greatest challenges in bioremediation is dealing with various

CREATING BIODEGRADABLE PLASTIC

Synthetic plastics do not break down naturally, and so they cause pollution problems. However, when certain bacteria are fed sugar, fats, or starch, they produce substances that resemble plastic. The bacteria store these plasticlike substances as energy sources.

Scientists can make the bacteria produce large amounts of the bioplastic. Under the right conditions other microorganisms break down the bioplastic within a few months. This helps reduce plastic pollution.

Knives, forks, and spoons made from a starch–polyester bioplastic material can be broken down by microorganisms.

MICROORGANISMS AND SEWAGE TREATMENT

The treatment of sewage usually involves several steps, most of which use microorganisms. After filtering out any large or nonbiodegradable particles, the raw sewage is piped into basins where aerobic (oxygen-using) microorganisms, such as bacteria, fungi, and protozoa, reduce the amount of organic compounds. Most treatment systems are designed to keep the oxygen concentration of the sewage high enough to support a growing population of aerobic microorganisms and to provide plenty of surfaces that microorganisms can attach to. Sewage is often trickled or sprayed over these surfaces to allow maximum contact between the sewage and the microorganisms, and to keep the dissolved oxygen in the liquid at a high level.

PERCOLATING FILTER METHOD

Sewage drips onto filter beds.

rotating sprinkler

clinker (fused stony matter) and stones covered in microorganisms

untreated sewage

Treated sewage is discharged into a river.

ACTIVATED SLUDGE METHOD

untreated sewage

Air bubbles add oxygen and mix sewage and sludge.

activated sludge, rich in microorganisms

treated sewage

sludge

treated and sold

and plastics. Such compounds are so new to the environment that microorganisms have not yet developed ways to break them down. Sometimes scientists can genetically alter microorganisms to increase their ability to do so. These GM microorganisms often grow well in the presence of the pollutant but die when they start to run out of food and have to compete with naturally occurring microorganisms. Scientists release GM microorganisms into the environment only when other methods have failed, because of the unpredicted side effects such introductions may have.

This kind of bioremediation has been practiced for only a few decades; but another form of bioremediation, the biological treatment of sewage, has been used for about 100 years. In two methods of treating sewage

chemical compounds that do not occur naturally. They include some artificial industrial solvents, pesticides, detergents,

WORKING TOWARD IMMUNITY

Immunization helps the body fight invaders before they cause disease. An early form of immunization, called variolation, was practiced in the 10th century by Chinese healers. They noticed that people who survived smallpox were immune to the disease. They tried to transfer immunity from smallpox survivors to people who had never had the disease. By the 16th century they had developed a workable technique. Scabs from smallpox survivors were dried, ground up, and blown into the nostrils of healthy people. Most treated people developed only a mild form of smallpox and were then completely immune to it.

The French chemist Louis Pasteur (1822–1895) successfully inoculated healthy chickens with cholera bacteria to immunize them against chicken cholera. To inoculate means to introduce the organism to the skin surface rather than injecting it.

Pasteur also looked for a cure for the disease anthrax, which kills cows and sheep. He tested these animals with anthrax cultures. Other scientists did not believe that Pasteur's method would work, but he was proved right. Untreated animals died, but those that had been immunized did not develop anthrax.

All inoculation cultures are called vaccines. There are vaccines against diseases such as typhoid, cholera, plague, and tuberculosis. These vaccines are usually given by injection, but some are given to subjects orally.

microorganisms take organic (carbon-containing) materials from waste water. Treated water can be returned safely to rivers and streams.

ADVANCEMENT OF BIOTECHNOLOGY

Microbiologists doing research work on modern medicines use microorganisms to make many life-saving products, such as vaccines, antibiotics, and certain vitamins and drugs called steroids. Scientists around the world are searching for these valuable microorganisms.

Lady Montagu (1689–1762) introduced smallpox variolation to Britain after witnessing it in Turkey, where she lived.

Microorganisms, especially fungi and bacteria, produce antibiotics. The antibiotics can kill off competition from rival bacteria. Modern medicine relies heavily on antibiotics because they are the only

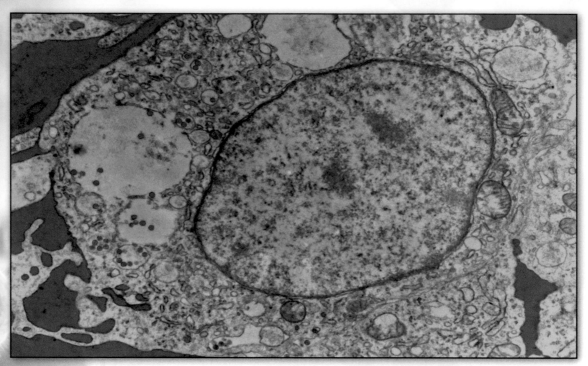

The avian leukosis virus is shown here (in red) in the limb buds of a 9-day-old chicken embryo. This retrovirus can lead to cancer in chickens and possibly infect other species of animals.

known cure for many infectious diseases, both of people and of farm animals. For about 50 years cattle, pig, and chicken farmers have put low doses of antibiotics into livestock feed to help prevent disease and promote growth.

However, people are now increasingly worried that antibiotic use in farming may be breeding drug-resistant microorganisms. Low doses of antibiotics given to livestock on a daily basis may not kill all the microorganisms, allowing resistant strains to build up over time. Resistant microorganisms could pass on their antibiotic-resistant genes to microorganisms that cause human diseases, making people more vulnerable to serious infections.

CREATING INSULIN

Insulin is a hormone that controls the amount of sugar in the blood. It is produced by an organ called the pancreas. Too little insulin production leads to a disorder called diabetes. Diabetes is treated by injections of insulin taken from the pancreas of cattle. But insulin taken from cows can cause allergic reactions in people. So, a form of insulin produced by genetically engineered bacteria is also used. Synthetic insulin is made by inserting the human gene for the hormone into bacteria such as *Escherichia coli. E. coli* are put in a large tank called a bioreactor to multiply, after which the insulin is extracted.

These gas pumps offer biodiesel, which is derived from the oil in plants like soybeans and corn. Some argue that biodiesel is more sustainable than fossil fuels.

Microorganisms also make many other products besides vaccines and antibiotics. By inserting human DNA into microorganisms, genetic engineers have succeeded in making them produce human proteins and hormones. Some of these drugs, such as interferon and tumor necrosis factor (TNF), appear to help the body's immune system fight viruses and cancer.

CREATING FUEL

Microorganisms can make several useful fuels, including ethanol, methane, and hydrogen. In most parts of the world it is currently still cheaper and easier to use petroleum. But as the world's petroleum supply shrinks, people will soon have to use alternative fuels. Fossil fuels such as petroleum pollute the atmosphere. For that reason alone, people are researching alternative fuels. The best fuel-producing microorganisms are those that make a lot of fuel but do not cost much to feed. Microorganisms that live on a diet of waste, such as sewage, garbage, or industrial wastes, are good candidates.

BACTERIA AND COPPER MINING

Much of the world's copper is mined with the help of bacteria. Just as many other metals are, copper is often embedded in deep layers of sulfide deposits. A solution of sulfuric acid is sprayed onto the copper ore to encourage sulfur-oxidizing bacteria to separate the copper from the sulfide mixture. Similar processes are used to mine other metals such as gold, lead, nickel, and cobalt.

HEATING MARS

With an average annual temperature of −67 °F (−55 °C), Mars (below) is too cold for people to live there. Scientists are looking at ways of warming Mars by creating an artificial greenhouse effect. Methane-producing bacteria called methanogens could be introduced to Mars' surface. Methane is a powerful greenhouse gas that traps heat. Research has shown that methanogens can grow in an environment like that of Mars. Perhaps methanogens on Mars will one day warm the planet for people.

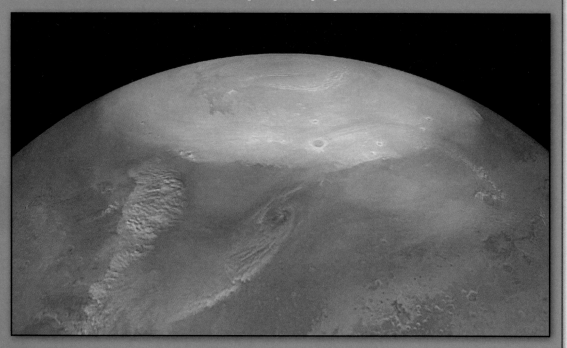

This NASA photo clearly shows the polar ice cap on Mars, which is currently far too cold for human inhabitants.

When certain yeasts are fed sugar from grains or agricultural wastes such as leaves and stems, for example, they change it to an alcohol called ethanol by the process of fermentation. Ethanol has long been used in the production of alcoholic beverages. It is increasingly being used in gasohol, which is 90 percent unleaded gasoline and 10 percent ethanol.

In the absence of oxygen some bacteria produce a mixture of carbon dioxide, methane, and other gases called biogas. They do so as they digest wastes containing a lot of organic material, such as animal manure. Biogas usually contains about 55 to 80 percent methane, which can be burned to generate electricity and heat or used as fuel for cars and buses.

CHAPTER SEVEN

BIOGRAPHY: LOUIS PASTEUR

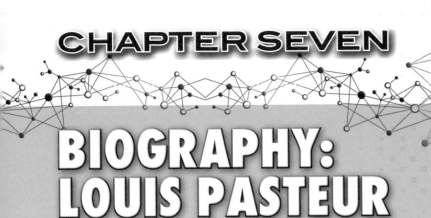

Countless lives have been saved thanks to the work of French chemist Louis Pasteur. Among many other contributions to science, he proved that infectious diseases are caused by microscopic organisms called germs, and developed ways of treating them. He invented the process of "pasteurization" and introduced vaccines for potentially fatal diseases such as anthrax and rabies.

Louis Pasteur was born on December 27, 1822, in Dole, Jura, in eastern France, the son of a tanner. The family soon moved to the small town of Arbois, near Dole, where in 1829 Louis entered the Collège Communal. He was not a brilliant pupil, but he had a talent for painting and his ambition was to become an art teacher.

In 1838 Pasteur attended the Royal College in the city of Besançon, eastern France, graduating in arts in 1840 and in science in 1842, though he only managed a "mediocre" for chemistry at that time. The same summer he took his entrance exam for the École Normale Supérieure, a college in Paris for training teachers. Pasteur was very disappointed when he came in only 15th out of 22 in the exam. However, he was hardworking and focused, so he decided to study for another year and take the exam again. This time he came

Louis Pasteur, French chemist and microbiologist, is credited for discovering the causes and creating vaccines for several diseases that were widespread during his time.

KEY DATES

1822	Born on December 27 in Dole, Jura, eastern France
1829	Enters college in Arbois
1838–42	Attends the Royal College at Besançon; graduates in arts in 1840 and in science in 1842
1843	Admitted to École Normale Supérieure; attends lectures at the Sorbonne, University of Paris
1847	Graduates as a doctor of science
1848	Appointed professor of physics at the Dijon Lycée; then deputy professor of chemistry at the University of Strasbourg
1848	Experiments on the structure of racemic and tartaric acid crystals
1849	Marries Marie Laurent
1854	Becomes dean of chemistry at the University of Lille
1856	Awarded the Rumford medal of the Royal Society in London; begins investigating fermentation and putrefaction
1857	Becomes director of scientific studies at the École Normale Supérieure
1862	Elected to the French Academy of Sciences
1868	Discovers the cause of diseases in silkworms
1873	Becomes member of the French Academy of Medicine
1880	Develops a vaccine for chicken cholera
1881	Is elected to the French Academy
1882	Begins research into rabies
1885	Successfully inoculates his young patient Joseph Meister against rabies
1887	Becomes secretary of the French Academy of Sciences
1888	The Pasteur Institute opens in Paris
1889	Becomes director of the Pasteur Institute
1895	Dies at Saint-Cloud, near Paris, on September 28, and is given a state funeral

in fourth. Pasteur graduated as a doctor in 1847.

PASTEUR'S EARLY SUCCESS

Pasteur's early interests lay in the field of crystallography, which is the study of the structure of crystals.

He carried out detailed research into tartaric acid crystals, which he discovered have particular qualities when transmitting polarized light (light in which the wave vibrations are arranged in a single plane). This work laid the foundations for an important new branch of science called stereochemistry (the way atoms are arranged in molecules).

He met and married the daughter of the rector of the University of Strasbourg, Marie Laurent.

THE BIOLOGY OF BEER AND WINE

In 1854 Pasteur became dean and professor of chemistry at the newly founded University of Lille in northern France. An important local industry there was the production of alcohol from beets or grain, and it was in the course of visits to local factories that Pasteur became interested in fermentation, the process that changes sugars in certain foodstuffs into alcohol. Yeast is a type of fungus, and is used in brewing beer; at the time people believed fermentation was a purely chemical process, helped by the death and decomposition of the yeast cells. However, Pasteur discovered that fermentation is a biological process; in other words, that the "live" yeast was causing fermentation by actively feeding

Pasteur at work at the École Normale Supérieure, the teachers' college in Paris. The French emperor Napoleon III (1808–1873) helped finance the setting-up of Pasteur's chemistry laboratory there.

ROBERT KOCH
1843–1910

Robert Koch was a German bacteriologist and one of the founders of bacteriology (the study of bacteria). He established the laboratory techniques that are used to culture, stain, and observe bacteria. In 1882 he discovered the bacillus (a type of bacterium) responsible for causing the disease tuberculosis (TB), which usually affects the lungs. His later attempt to produce an inoculation against TB failed, however. He also discovered the bacillus responsible for causing the acute infection of the intestines, cholera.

Koch proposed four tests that a diagnosis must pass if it is to establish a link between a disease and an infection by a microorganism. These are usually known as "Koch's postulates," and are: 1. Specific living parasites must be found and identified in all or most of the samples taken from the host (it is not enough for them to be present in just a few specimens); 2. When isolated from the samples, these organisms must be capable of living independently; 3. The organisms must be able to survive when introduced into healthy tissue; 4. Once they are established in the healthy tissue, the symptoms of the disease must occur again in precisely their original form.

on sugars and producing alcohol as well as carbon dioxide gas.

In 1856 a local industrialist asked Pasteur to investigate why wine and beer sometimes turn sour. Examining good and sour beer under a microscope, Pasteur found that the good beer contained round yeast cells and the sour beer contained

Edité par la CHOCOLATERIE D'AIGUEBELLE (Monastère de la Trappe-Drôme)

PASTEUR DÉCOUVRE LA LOI DES FERMENTS

"Pasteur discovers the law of fermentation" proclaims the caption on a chocolate manufac-turer's promotional advertisement praising the achievements of French science. It shows Pasteur with students from the University of Lille. A local industrialist is impressed by his evidence that fermentation is a biological process caused by microorganisms such as yeasts and bacteria.

long and narrow (rodlike) yeast cells. Clearly there were two types of yeast. In the sour beer the yeast that produced alco-hol was being contaminated by other yeast cells to produce acetic acid (vinegar).

Pasteur discovered that souring could be prevented by gently heating beer or wine to 122°F (50°C), then sealing the container. Heating kills all the yeast, including the rodlike variety that would otherwise continue to make acetic acid while the drink was maturing.

Pasteur suspected that the yeast that made acetic acid must have entered the beer from the air. Eventually Pasteur was able to show that microorganisms carried in the air were responsible for the change that caused foods to fer-ment (change to alcohol) or to putrefy (rot and decay). Pasteurization, the pro-cess of controlled heating named after Pasteur, kills off these microorganisms, and is widely used in the food indus-try today to preserve foods. Milk is

MICROORGANISMS AND DEAD MATTER

Up until the 19th century, there were people who believed that, given the right conditions, low forms of life such as maggots and grubs were created from nonliving material, a theory that was known as spontaneous generation. Around 1600, for example, the Flemish physician and alchemist Jan Baptiste van Helmont (1577–1644) claimed that mice are produced naturally in dirty wheat.

In 1688 the Italian physician and poet Francesco Redi (1626–1697) performed an experiment with the aim of disproving this, arguing instead that all organisms develop from eggs that are too small to be seen. He prepared eight flasks containing different meats, four of them sealed and four open to the air. Flies landed on the meat exposed to the air and, in due course, maggots appeared. The meat in the closed flasks was no less rotten, but there were no maggots. Redi repeated the experiment, this time leaving

Pasteur's experiments disproved the theory of spontaneous generation, and proved that a heat-sterilized infusion could remain sterile if it were contained in a flask with a U-shaped bend in its neck. Even if the neck remained open, any germs would be trapped in the flask's U-bend.

THE SILKWORM CONNECTION

In the 1860s the French silk industry was being devastated by a disease that killed silkworms, which are the larvae or immature

pasteurized, for example, to destroy the bacteria that form lactic acid.

all eight flasks unsealed except by gauze: this allowed air, but not flies, to enter. Again the meat became putrid, but there were no maggots. This suggested that the maggots developed from tiny eggs laid on the meat by flies, rather than from the rotting meat itself, as previously thought.

PASTEUR AND NONLIVING MATTER

Pasteur boiled an infusion to make it sterile, and placed it in a number of flasks, which he sealed. He then opened some in the countryside and others high on a mountain before resealing them. After a time, microorganisms appeared in the flasks that had been opened in the countryside, but not in those opened on the mountain, where the air was much purer. All had been exposed to oxygen, but Pasteur showed that living organisms (germs) had to be present for sterile liquid to produce life forms.

In his second experiment, Pasteur placed boiled infusions in flasks with narrow U-shaped necks. Despite leaving them open to the air, no organisms appeared, because any germs were trapped in the U-bend. If the flask were tilted so that the liquid came into contact with the U-bend, organisms would appear in the infusion. So Pasteur proved that life does not arise from nonliving matter.

form of a species of moth. In June 1865 Pasteur accepted a commission from the government to investigate the problem. By 1868 he announced that he had found the insects were suffering from two separate diseases, both caused by tiny parasites. Parasites live in or on other animals or plants, known as hosts, and get their nourishment from them. Pasteur found these parasites present in the debris of the mulberry leaves on which the silkworms fed, and in the bodies of infected silkworms.

Combining this discovery with his work on fermentation and putrefaction, Pasteur went on to develop the germ theory of disease. Previously people had believed that disease was spread by poisonous fumes, known as miasma, that rose up from dung heaps and decaying material. Blown by the wind, the miasma could carry disease from one area to another. Pasteur's new theory, that disease was caused by microorganisms, gave people hope that these organisms could somehow be prevented from invading human bodies.

STUDY OF RABIES

Pasteur began one of his most famous pieces of research in 1882, in which he aimed to find a way of combating rabies. Rabies is a disease that can be passed from infected dogs or other animals to humans through a bite; symptoms include fear of water, throat convulsions, and paralysis; once symptoms

INFECTIOUS DISEASE

Pasteur showed that many diseases are caused when the body is infected by microscopically small airborne organisms. Since Pasteur's day, scientists have identified four main groups of disease-causing organisms that can infect both plants and animals.

PARASITIC BACTERIA AND PROTISTS

There are thousands of types of the single-celled microorganisms known as bacteria, but only a few are able to invade other organisms. Some of these may survive in a relationship with their host that is beneficial; for example, some bacteria live in the human digestive tract and help us to digest our food. However, illness can occur when the invading bacteria trigger a strong defensive response and the body's immune system tries to destroy them. This usually means the bacteria are trying to reproduce rapidly inside the body of the host. Some bacteria also release poisons that harm the host. Food poisoning, blood poisoning, tuberculosis, and anthrax are among the diseases caused by bacteria.

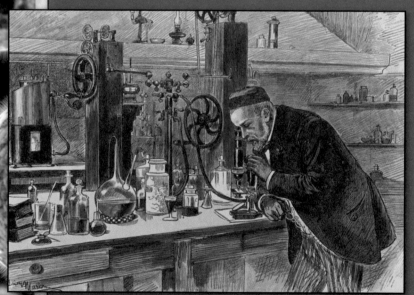

Protozoan parasites are also single-celled, but they are much bigger than bacteria. The cell has a wall with two layers and one or more nuclei containing the genetic material. Like all parasites they gain their nourishment from the host that they live on or in. Amoebic dysentery, sleeping sickness, and malaria are all diseases caused by protozoa.

FUNGAL INFECTION

Fungi occur as yeasts or molds. Fewer than 100 species are capable of invading animals, and very few of them can cause fatal diseases. Some infections are internal, but the most common fungal diseases affect the skin. Fungal diseases affecting humans include ringworm, athlete's foot, and thrush.

The flu virus as shown under a modern microscope. The flu virus is colored orange, while the cell being attacked is green.

VIRAL INFECTIONS

Viruses, the smallest and simplest of the infective organisms, were not known to exist until the early 20th century. They are so small they can be viewed only by use of an electron microscope. A virus consists of nucleic acid that is enclosed in a protective shell made from protein. It infects an organism by injecting its nucleic acid into a cell, where it incorporates itself into the cell's nucleus and then instructs the cell to make copies of itself. The cell then dies, releasing the viruses to invade more cells, and so on. The common cold, influenza, hepatitis, rabies, and AIDS are among the diseases caused by viruses.

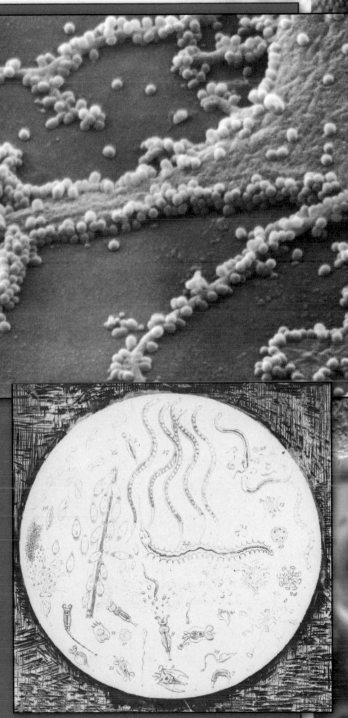

The realization that epidemic diseases might be caused by microorganisms—and not, as had previously been thought, by the unpleasant fumes known as miasma—encouraged careful examination of water supplies and attempts to halt the spread of germs. A 19th-century drawing (right) shows a range of microorganisms in drinking water; bacteria carried by water could cause typhoid and cholera.

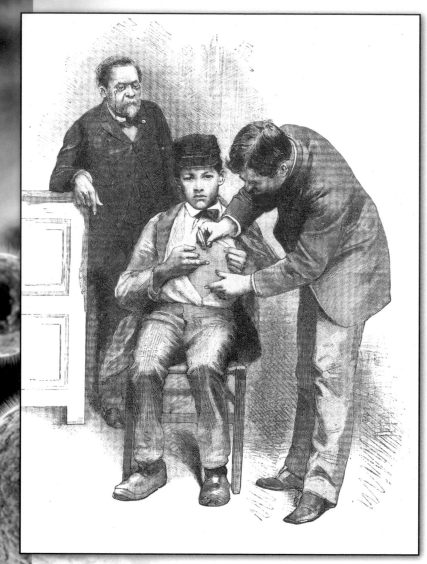

Pasteur watches as nine-year-old Joseph Meister is successfully inoculated against rabies, a deadly disease passed on in bites from infected animals.

disease—in fact it is a virus, though they had not yet been discovered—was present in the central nervous system (brain and spinal column). Eventually he developed a weakened form of the infection that he could use for inoculation.

Pasteur had successfully treated animals with his vaccine, but his work was still at an experimental stage when he was unexpectedly presented with a human subject. On July 6, 1885, the mother of Joseph Meister, a nine-year-old boy who had been badly bitten by a dog with rabies, begged Pasteur to inoculate him. Since the boy would almost certainly have died within a month, Pasteur agreed to try out his vaccine. Joseph Meister was saved, and since then the Pasteur vaccine has been used to prevent the onset of rabies in many thousands of people who have been infected.

THE PASTEUR INSTITUTE

The success of his rabies vaccine brought Pasteur great fame. He had

appear, the disease is usually fatal. After experimenting with inoculations made from the saliva of animals infected with rabies (which did not work), Pasteur concluded that the germ responsible for the

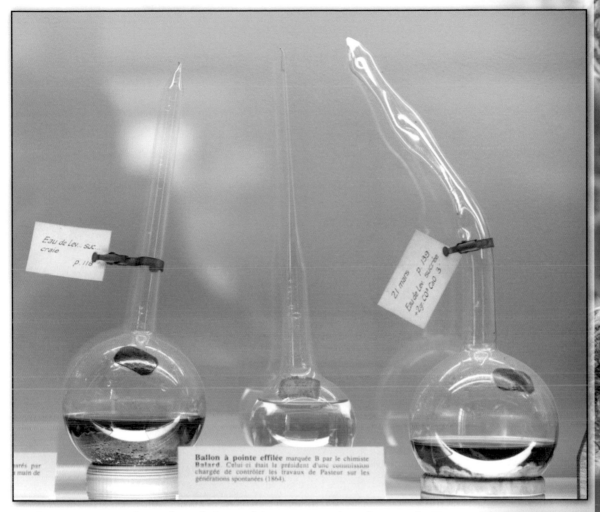

The instruments shown here belonged to Pasteur and are kept at the Pasteur Museum in France. They were used for his study of fermentation and spontaneous generation.

been made a member of the French Academy of Medicine in 1873, and in 1874 the French National Assembly awarded him a pension for life. Many people regarded Pasteur as a national hero, and the public raised money to help Pasteur in his work; in 1888 the Pasteur Institute opened in Paris. This was a private research laboratory dedicated to investigating rabies further and preventing its spread; branches followed in other parts of France and elsewhere. Louis Pasteur remained as director of the institute until he died at Saint-Cloud, near Paris, on September 28, 1895.

SCIENTIFIC BACKGROUND

Before 1820

Dutch scientist Anton van Leeuwenhoek (1632–1723) observes "animalcules" (bacteria)

English physician Edward Jenner (1749–1823) develops a vaccine for use against smallpox

1820

1823 Edward Jenner dies on January 26, a month after Pasteur's birth

1830

1838 German physiologist Theodor Schwann (1810–1882) shows that yeast is composed of tiny living organisms; it is only Pasteur's later work that will convince scientists this is true

1840 German anatomist Friedrich Gustav Jakob Henle (1809–1885) suggests diseases are caused by microorganisms

1840

1848 Pasteur publishes his research on stereoisomers of racemic acid

1848 Hungarian obstetrician Ignaz Philipp Semmelweiss (1818–1865) introduces antiseptic methods into a Viennese maternity hospital; death rates fall dramatically

1850

1854 English epidemiologist John Snow (1813–1858) discovers that cholera is transmitted through contaminated water

1856 Pasteur begins research into the process of fermentation

1860

1865 English surgeon Joseph Lister (1827–1912) introduces carbolic acid as an antiseptic in hospitals

1868 Pasteur rescues the silkworm industry by discovering cause of silkworm diseases flacherie and pébrine

1870

1873 Pasteur is elected to the French Academy of Medicine

1876 German physician Robert Koch (1843–1910) identifies the bacterium that causes anthrax

1880

1880 Pasteur develops a vaccine against chicken cholera

1885 On July 6 Pasteur successfully inoculates Joseph Meister against rabies

1883 Koch isolates the cause of cholera

1890

1890 German and Japanese bacteriologists Emil Adolf von Behring (1854–1917) and Shibasabura Kitasato (1852–1931) discover diphtheria antitoxin serum

1898 Dutch botanist Martinus Beijerinck (d. 1931) discovers that tobacco mosaic disease is caused by an organism that is not a bacterium; he calls it a virus

1900

After 1900

1906 Belgian physiologist Jules Jean Baptiste Vincent Bordet (1870–1961) discovers the bacterium that causes whooping cough

1910 German bacteriologist Paul Ehrlich (1854–1915) uses salvarsan, the first antibacterial drug, in tests to treat syphilis

POLITICAL AND CULTURAL BACKGROUND

1815 French emperor Napoleon Bonaparte (1769–1821) is defeated at the battle of Waterloo in Belgium by British, Dutch, and German troops; he abdicates four days later

1820 *Lamia and Other Poems* by English poet John Keats (1795–1821) is published; it includes great works such as his odes "To Autumn," "On a Grecian Urn," and "To a Nightingale"

1824 Charles X (1757–1836) succeeds to the throne of France and attempts to restore the absolute power of the monarchy; he is overthrown in the revolution of July 27–29, 1830

1835 In Paris the Arc de Triomphe, the triumphal arch commissioned by Napoleon in 1806, is completed

1844 French writer Alexandre Dumas (1802–1870) completes his novels *The Count of Monte Cristo* and *The Three Musketeers*

1885 On July 6 Pasteur successfully inoculates Joseph Meister against rabies

1883 Koch isolates the cause of cholera

1890

1890 German and Japanese bacteriologists Emil Adolf von Behring (1854–1917) and Shibasabura Kitasato (1852–1931) discover diphtheria antitoxin serum

1900

1898 Dutch botanist Martinus Beijerinck (d. 1931) discovers that tobacco mosaic disease is caused by an organism that is not a bacterium; he calls it a virus

After 1900

1906 Belgian physiologist Jules Jean Baptiste Vincent Bordet (1870–1961) discovers the bacterium that causes whooping cough

1910 German bacteriologist Paul Ehrlich (1854–1915) uses salvarsan, the first antibacterial drug, in tests to treat syphilis

aerobic respiration Production of energy in the presence of oxygen.

anaerobic respiration Production of energy in the absence of oxygen.

antibiotic A drug that kills bacteria.

antibody Protein produced by white blood cells in response to an antigen; important in an immune response.

antigen Molecule on a foreign body that the immune system can recognize.

asexual reproduction Production of young without the need for mating or the fusion of sex cells.

bacteriophage Virus that attacks bacteria.

bacterium A single-celled organism that lacks a nucleus and organelles.

binary fission Form of asexual reproduction in single-celled organisms; one cell divides into two.

bioluminescence The production of light by living organisms.

bioremediation The use of microorganisms to clean up pollution spills.

biotechnology Industrial uses for microorganisms.

capsid Protein shell that protects the genetic material of a virus.

chemoautotroph Organism that uses chemicals such as sulfides to make food.

chlorophyll Green pigment essential for photosynthesis that occurs inside chloroplasts.

cilium Small filament that occurs in banks on cells to allow them to move.

conjugation A one-way transfer of DNA between bacteria.

cytoplasm Region of a cell that lies outside the nucleus.

deoxyribonucleic acid (DNA) Molecule that contains the genetic code for all cellular (nonvirus) organisms.

enzyme Protein that speeds up chemical reactions inside an organism.

epidemic A major outbreak of a disease.

eukaryote cell Cell of a plant, animal, fungus, or protist; contains structures called organelles.

fermentation Process that uses microorganisms to break down sugars into simpler molecules, such as alcohol.

fimbria One of many hairlike extensions of a bacterial cell that keep it attached to a surface or to another cell.

flagellum Long filament used by many single-celled organisms to get around.

food vacuole Small organelle inside an ameba inside which digestion of food takes place.

gene Section of DNA (or RNA in some viruses) that codes for the structure of a protein.

Gram stain Technique used to identify bacteria; a dye stains bacteria purple, but only if significant amounts of a chemical, peptidoglycan, occur in their outer layer.

halophile Bacterium that lives in very salty conditions.

heterotroph Organism (such as an animal) that gets food by eating other organisms.

hydrothermal vent A crack in rocks deep under the sea from which streams of very hot, chemical-laden water well up from inside the Earth's crust.

junk DNA Long section of noncoding DNA that serves no apparent function; occurs in some archaebacteria.

mutation A change in a cell's DNA.

mutualism A relationship to the mutual benefit of two or more species.

nitrate Compound that contains nitrogen and oxygen; one of the products of the nitrogen- fixation process.

nitrogen fixation The incorporation by soil bacteria of nitrogen in the air into nitrate compounds that plants are able to use.

nucleus Organelle that contains a eukaryote cell's DNA.

organelle Membrane-lined structures inside eukaryote cells, such as the chloroplasts.

osmosis The movement of water through a membrane from points of high to low concentration.

pandemic Massive outbreak of a disease that can sweep across continents or even the whole world.

pathogen An organism that causes disease.

photoautotroph Organism that uses the energy of the sun to make food.

photosynthesis The conversion of water and carbon dioxide into sugars in plants, using the energy of sunlight.

phytoplankton Plantlike algae that float in the surface waters of lakes or the ocean.

pilus Hairlike structure produced by a bacterium during conjugation. DNA moves through the pilus from one cell to the other.

plasmid Ring of DNA separate from a bacterium's main genetic material.

prion A protein that does not contain DNA or RNA but can cause diseases.

prokaryote cell Cell of an organism that does not contain organelles.

protist A single-celled organism with a nucleus and organelles.

pseudopod Extension of an ameba into which the rest of the cell can flow, allowing movement.

ribonucleic acid (RNA) Chemical similar to DNA that is involved in protein production.

ribosome Granule on which protein production occurs.

sexual reproduction Production of young through the fusion of sex cells, often after mating between a male and a female.

symbiosis A relationship between different organisms.

thermophile Bacterium that can live at very high temperatures.

trichocyst Harpoonlike structure fired from beneath the outer layer of ciliates; used for anchorage or to inject toxins into other organisms.

vaccine Dead or harmless versions of a disease-causing organism that are injected into the body. It allows the immune system to recognize the pathogen.

viroid Organism formed by a single RNA molecule folded into a complex three-dimensional shape.

zooplankton Small animals that float in the surface waters of lakes or the ocean.

American Association for the
Advancement of Science
1200 New York Avenue NW
Washington, DC 20005
(202) 326-6400
Web site: http://www.aaas.org
An international nonprofit organization
dedicated to advancing science
around the world by serving as an
educator, leader, spokesperson, and
professional association.

American Museum of Natural History
Central Park West at 79th Street
New York, NY 10024-5192
(212) 769-5100
Web site: http://www.amnh.org
Museum showcasing hundreds of ani-
mal species and fossils from the
history of life on Earth.

Centers for Disease Control and
Prevention
1600 Clifton Road
Atlanta, GA 30333
(800) CDC-INFO
Web site: http://www.cdc.gov
Organization whose goal is prevention of
disease, creating awareness, promoting
heath and prevention strategies, and
training people in the medical field.

New York Hall of Science
47-01 111th Street
Queens, NY 11368-2950
Web site: http://www.nysci.org
E-mail: info@nysci.org
A hands-on science and technology cen-
ter that offers visitors the chance to

participate in activities while learn-
ing about science.

The Science Museum
Exhibition Road
South Kensington
SW7 2DD
London UK
Web site: http://www.sciencemuseum
.org.uk
Science museum renowned for its col-
lections, galleries, and exhibitions
dedicated to science.

World Health Organization
Avenue Appia 20
1211 Geneva 27
Switzerland
Web site: http://www.who.int
The directing and coordinating authority
for health within the United Nations
system. It is responsible for providing
leadership on global health matters,
shaping the health research agenda,
setting norms and standards, articulat-
ing evidence-based policy options,
providing technical support to countries, and monitoring and assessing
health trends.

WEB SITES

Due to the changing nature of Internet
links, Rosen Publishing has developed an
online list of Web sites related to the subject
of this book. This site is updated regularly.
Please use this link to access the list:

http://www.rosenlinks.com/CORE/Micro

Bailey, Diane. *Cholera*. New York, NY: Rosen Publishing, 2010.

Bailey, Diane. *The Plague*. New York, NY: Rosen Publishing, 2010.

Fandel, Jennifer. *Louis Pasteur and Pasteurization*. North Mankato, MN: Capstone, 2010.

Furgang, Adam. *Smallpox*. New York, NY: Rosen Publishing, 2010.

Hyde, Natalie. *Micro Life in Soil*. New York, NY: Crabtree, 2010.

Jones, Molly. *AIDS*. New York, NY: Rosen Publishing, 2010.

Kornberg, Arthur. *Germ Stories*. Herndon, VA: University Science Books, 2007.

Miles, Liz. *Louis Pasteur*. North Mankato, MN: Heinemann-Raintree, 2008.

Murphy, Jim. *Invincible Microbe: Tuberculosis and the Never-ending Search for the Cure*. New York, NY: Houghton Mifflin, 2012.

Ollhoff, Jim. *The Germ Detectives*. Minneapolis, MN: ABDO, 2009.

Orr, Tamra. *Public Health Microbiologist*. New York, NY: Gareth Stevens, 2007.

Orr, Tamra B. *Polio*. New York, NY: Rosen Publishing, 2010.

Snedden, Robert. *The Benefits of Bacteria*. North Mankato, MN: Heinemann-Raintree, 2007.

Snedden, Robert. *The World of Microorganisms*. North Mankato, MN: Heinemann-Raintree, 2007.

Stimola, Aubrey. *Ebola*. New York, NY: Rosen Publishing, 2010.

Swanson, Jennifer Ann. *Uninvited Guests: Invisible Creatures Lurking in Your Home*. North Mankato, MN: Capstone, 2011.

Zamosky, Lisa. *Louis Pasteur: Founder of Microbiology*. North Mankato, MN: Compass Point Books, 2008.

A

aerobic bacteria, 14
AIDS/HIV, 7, 8, 34, 38, 39, 40, 42–43, 46, 47, 48, 50, 52, 53, 57, 81
algae, 7, 8, 9, 22, 23, 24, 26, 27, 30, 31
amebas, 7, 22, 24, 25, 27, 32
anaerobic bacteria, 13, 15
anthrax, 46, 47, 48, 57, 66, 69, 73, 80
antibiotics, 56–57, 69–70, 71
   resistance to, 17, 18, 20, 57, 62, 70
antibodies, 51, 52, 54
antiseptics, 54
antivirals, 57
archaebacteria, 12, 13–14, 15, 18, 25
asexual reproduction, 19, 20, 29
athlete's foot, 46, 80
autotrophs, 15–16

B

Bacillus thuringiensis (Bt), 65
bacteria
   and copper mining, 71
   and disease, 6, 7, 10, 20–21
   DNA, 16–18
   and the food industry, 12
   and the Gram stain, 17
   groups, 14
   measurements, 11–12
   movement, 19
   and nutrients, 15–16
   and oil spills, 66
   reproduction, 19–20
   and resistance to antibiotics, 17, 18, 20, 57, 62, 70
   structure, 16
   types, 12–15
bacteriophages, 45, 64
baculoviruses, 40

beer brewing, 60
binary fission, 18, 20
biogas, 72
bioluminescence, 26
bioplastic/biodegradable plastic, 67
bioremediation, 67–69
biotechnology, 9, 59, 69–71
bioterrorism, 66
Black Death, 48

C

capsid, 38, 40
cell division, 29
cell membrane, 16, 28, 40
cell wall, 16, 57
Chagas' disease, 31, 32, 33
cheesemaking, 9, 12, 61
chemoautotrophs, 15, 16
chicken pox, 42
chlorophyll, 27
chloroplasts, 19
cholera, 10, 21, 46, 48, 54, 56, 69, 76
cilia, 28
ciliates, 24, 25, 26, 27, 28, 30
common cold, 41, 81
compost, making your own, 9
computer viruses, 45
conjugation, 20
contractile vacuoles, 30
copper mining, bacteria and, 71
coral bleaching, 31
corals, 8, 31
Creutzfeldt-Jakob disease, 44
cyanobacteria, 14
cytoplasm, 16, 17, 18–19, 40

D

diabetes, 70
diatoms, 24, 25, 26, 30

dinoflagellates, 24, 26, 30, 31, 32
diphtheria, 46, 50
disease, microorganisms and
   fighting disease, 49–51
   four main groups of disease-causing
     organisms, 80–81
   germ theory of disease, development
     of, 79
   how disease is spread, 48–49
   pathogens, explanation of, 46–47
   preventing outbreaks, 54–57
   treatment of disease, 53–54
   treatment of viruses, 57
   vaccinating against disease, 52–53
DNA, 11, 15, 16–18, 20, 28, 34, 37, 38, 39,
     40, 44, 45, 57, 62, 63–64, 71
dysentery, 32, 80

E

Ebola virus, 43
Epulopiscium fischelsoni, 12
eubacteria, 12, 13, 14–15, 16, 20, 25
eukaryotes, 11, 15, 18, 19, 23, 25

F

fermentation, 7, 12, 59–60, 61, 72,
     74–77, 79
fimbriae, 19
flagella, 19, 28
Fleming, Alexander, 21
food industry, microorganisms and, 12,
     58, 59–60, 77
food vacuoles, 27
foraminiferans, 24, 25, 27
fossils, 14, 27, 35
fuels, alternative, 71–72
fungi, 6, 11, 12, 23, 25, 34, 46, 58, 59, 60,
     61, 68, 69, 74, 80

G

gasohol, 72
genetically modified crops/foods, 62, 63,
     64, 65, 66
genetic engineering, 9, 37, 58, 62, 63–66,
     69, 71
germ theory of disease, development
     of, 79
gonorrhea, 10
Gram, Hans Christian, 17
Gram stain, 17

H

halophile bacteria, 13, 14
Helmont, Jan Baptiste van, 78
hepatitis, 44, 52, 81
herpesvirus, 40, 42, 57
heterotrophs, 15, 16
HIV/AIDS, 7, 8, 34, 38, 39, 40, 42–43, 46,
     47, 48, 50, 52, 53, 57, 81
host cells, 34, 38, 39, 40, 43

I

incubation period, 48
induced immune response, 51
influenza, 8, 39, 42, 43, 46, 48, 50, 52, 81
insulin, 70
interferon, 71
introns, 18

J

Japanese beetle, 63
Jenner, Edward, 52

K

kelp, 25
kissing bugs, 31

Koch, Robert, 7, 49, 57, 76
Koch's postulates, 57, 76

L

Lactobacillus, 12, 61
Leeuwenhoek, Anton van, 7
Legionnaire's disease, 55
Leuconostoc, 12
Lister, Joseph, 54

M

mad cow disease, 44
malaria, 22, 32–33, 46, 55, 56, 80
Mars, 72
measles, 42, 43
medicine, cost of, 53
miasma, 79
microalgae, 7, 24
microbiology, explanation of, 6
microorganisms
  and biotechnology, 9, 59, 69–71
  explanation, 6
  and the food industry, 12, 58, 59–60, 77
  and fuel, 71–72
  and genetic engineering, 9, 37, 58, 62,
    63–66, 69, 71
  importance, 7–8
  and waste cleanup, 58, 66–69
  where they live, 6, 8–9
mitochondria, 19
mosquitoes, 32–33, 55
mutations, 18, 20
mutualism, 8
mycoprotein, 60

N

nitrogen fixation, 8, 11
nuclei, 11, 16–17, 23, 28, 40, 81

O

oil spills, bacteria and, 66
organelles, 18–19, 27
organic faming, 65
osmosis, 30

P

pandemics, 48
parasites/parasitic relationships, 8, 22,
    31, 32–33, 34, 35, 55, 79
Pasteur, Louis, 7, 49, 52, 69, 73–83
Pasteur Institute, 82–83
pasteurization, 55, 73, 77–78
pathogens, explanation of, 46–47
penicillin, 21, 57
phagocytes, 50
photoautotrophs, 15–16
photosynthesis, 7, 16, 19, 26–27, 28
pilus, 20
plague, 46, 48, 57, 66, 69
plankton, 7, 22, 30, 31
plasmids, 17–18, 57, 62–63, 64
plasmid vectors, 62
Plasmodium, 33
polio, 39, 42, 52
prions, 44
prokaryotes, 11, 25
protists
  classifying, 23
  collecting your own, 23
  defense, 27
  and the ecosystem, 22, 30–31
  fossils, 27
  movement, 28–29
  parasitic relationships, 32–33
  reproduction, 29
  structure and evolution, 22–26
  symbioses, 31
  types, 24
  what they eat, 26–27

pseudopods, 27
putrefaction/rotting, 7, 77, 79

Q

quinine, 56

R

rabies, 43, 52, 73, 79–82
radiolarians, 24, 25, 27, 31
Redi, Francesco, 78
reproduction
    asexual, 19, 20, 29
    of bacteria, 19–20
    of protists, 29
    sexual, 19, 28
    of viruses, 38–40
ribosomes, 18
ringworm, 80
RNA, 34, 36, 37, 38, 39, 44, 45

S

Salmonella, 21
secondary infections, 50
sewage treatment, 68
sexual reproduction, 19, 28
shingles, 42
sleeping sickness, 31, 32, 33, 52, 80
smallpox, 8, 34, 35, 37, 43, 46, 47,
    52–53, 69
Spanish flu, 48
spontaneous generation, 49, 78–79
Streptococcus, 12, 13, 61
Sulfolobus, 14, 16
symbioses, 8, 31
syphilis, 46, 47, 48

T

thermophile bacteria, 13, 14
thrush, 80
tobacco mosaic virus (TMV), 41
toxic blooms, 32
trichocysts, 27
Trichomonas, 32
trypanosomes, 31, 33
tuberculosis, 7, 10, 18, 21, 46, 55, 69,
    76, 80
tularemia, 66
tumor necrosis factor (TNF), 71
typhoid, 46, 48, 54, 69

V

vaccination/immunization, 44, 52–53
    history of, 52, 69
Valdez oil spill, 66
variolation, 69
Vibrio cholerae, 21
viroids, 36
viruses
    classification, 37
    and disease, 34, 39, 41–44
    and the environment, 44–45
    and plants, 41
    reproduction, 38–40
    structure, 38
    where they came from, 35

Y

yeast, 12, 58, 59, 60, 72, 74–77
yellow fever, 34, 42
yogurt, making your own, 13

Z

zooxanthellae, 31

PHOTO CREDITS